LISTS TO LOVE BY
FOR BUSY HUSBANDS

LISTS TO LOVE BY FOR BUSY HUSBANDS

Simple Steps to the Marriage You Want

Mark and Susan Merrill

New York Boston Nashville

FaithWords
Hachette Book Group
1290 Avenue of the Americas, New York, NY 10104
faithwords.com
twitter.com/faithwords

First Edition: January 2017

FaithWords is a division of Hachette Book Group, Inc. The FaithWords name and logo are trademarks of Hachette Book Group, Inc.

The publisher is not responsible for websites (or their content) that are not owned by the publisher.

The Hachette Speakers Bureau provides a wide range of authors for speaking events. To find out more, go to www.hachettespeakersbureau.com or call (866) 376-6591.

Library of Congress Cataloging-in-Publication Data has been applied for.

ISBN 978-1-4555-9683-6 (hardcover)—ISBN 978-1-4555-9684-3 (ebook)

Printed in the United States of America

LSC-C

10 9 8 7 6 5 4 3 2 1

To our sons, Mark Jr. and Grant; to our son-in-law, Hampton; and to every man who desires to love his wife well.

CONTENTS

Contents

Contents

INTRODUCTION

Before I married Susan, there were many things that attracted me to her. Two of those were her creativity and playfulness. She was very different from me. I was more disciplined and executed well on tasks. In many ways we are opposites. Before marriage opposites attract; however, many times after marriage, opposites attack. The things that once were cute and alluring can become the things that drive you the craziest.

Unfortunately, in my younger years, I thought pretty highly of myself. Early on in our marriage, I thought so much of myself that I thought Susan should be more like me. I wouldn't say that out loud, but I thought things like, "If Susan was more organized and disciplined like me, then she would be able to keep the house cleaner." Or, "I wish Susan just got things done that I want done when I want them done. I mean, when I commit to do something for her,

I'm on it and check it off the list." I became more and more critical of her.

Susan: *In my mind Mark was like an ice cream shop. It seemed like every week there was something he wanted me to work on or change about myself. I called it the flavor of the week because it was always different from last week but equally important. I'm a people pleaser, so I constantly felt as though I wasn't doing anything right. It was really hard for me to produce every "flavor" he wanted. I began to doubt myself, and my confidence was failing for the first time in my people-pleasing, overachieving life. After consistently being criticized I started to change and become more serious. I started to become more like Mark.*

Since I thought Susan should think and act more like me, I didn't think about the incredible gifts of creativity and relational skills that Susan had. I didn't celebrate the unique strengths that make Susan, Susan. When she ultimately became more like me, I was surprised to find that I didn't like it. I missed her. The last thing we needed was two of the same person. We make a much more powerful team when our unique gifts are brought together. We are much more complete. I don't need Susan to change. I need to love her for who she is. That has been the life's work of our marriage. It is learning how to love one another well.

The road has been long and challenging, but also good and full of joy. Susan would tell you that I am a different husband today than in those early days of marriage. Don't get me wrong—I am still a work in progress today and will continue to be, but I have become much better at loving my wife. Any improvement that has been made began with a decision. Most people in the world believe that love is a feeling. That may be partially true, but it's also a decision. Because I loved my wife I made a decision to change and, perhaps more important, show that change through my actions, attitudes, and words. The transformation has come little by little. Every day I attempt to take another step toward a better marriage. Unconditional love calls us to sacrifice and give selflessly whether or not we get anything in return. As a husband, that is what I am committed to living out.

But it's hard. Really hard. I continue to fall down and get up and try again the next day. Our fast-paced lives of schedules, obligations, technology, and financial burdens make loving each other well even more complicated. That's why we have broken down what we have learned into the lists in this book. No matter how busy you are, using it will help you love your wife well. Each day it will help you take the steps to love her more deeply when you feel like it and when you don't; when the love in your marriage is a two-way street and when it's a one-way street.

How do we know that these lists are vehicles to carry love into a marriage? For over two decades we've been writing and sharing marriage content. Our posts have received tens of millions of page views during that time.

A careful analysis of our Google Analytics reports, combined with our experiences over these years, tell us that there is a recurring theme with most of our high-ranking marriage posts. Each post addresses one or all of the following common denominators: expectations, evaluation, or improvements. People are searching for ways to manage their expectations, evaluate how they are doing, and improve their marriage. The lists in this book will help you to do that conveniently and consistently. You are going to be tasked with understanding your expectations and how they have affected your marriage. Second, you will be asked to evaluate yourself and your marriage. Third, you'll be challenged to make improvements, however small or large, with each list.

Expectations

We all bring expectations into marriage and develop expectations during the marriage. Our personalities, upbringing, experiences, and influences all shape those expectations. I had many expectations for Susan and myself that needed to change.

And that is the goal—to change the expectations that need to change. To do that we will have to answer some great questions. The big question is: *What do I expect?* Other questions include: *Are my expectations realistic? Are they fair? What should I expect of myself in marriage? What should I expect of my wife?*

Evaluation

In his book *Leadership Is an Art*, former CEO Max De Pree says that "the first responsibility of a leader is to define reality." We need to stop and measure ourselves. We need to take the time to assess the track we are on before it becomes a runaway train. *How are we doing as a couple, relationally?* That's one question you need to answer, but you also need to have a clear understanding of how your wife feels about your relationship. Does she feel connected, loved, and supported?

Most of the time, couples measure themselves against a very subjective standard: other people and other couples. It's called comparison. The problem with doing so is that others are always an unknown target. We never know what's really going on behind the closed curtains of their lives, and we don't know whether they are even pursuing a true standard. Thus, couples need an objective standard to measure against. One that is always true. God is truth and His revealed, God-breathed Word is completely true. In our lists to love by we always strive to communicate God's precepts and principles for marriage. When people evaluate against God's standards, either their existing expectations will be reinforced or negated, or a new expectation will be created.

Improvements

Once you know what you should expect and have evaluated how you both see your marriage, you can pursue the answer to the question: *How can we do this better?* Couples crave love. If you are reading this book you most likely want to love and be loved. You want a more intimate and fulfilling union. The best place to start is by asking: *How can I do this better? What should I do? What should I say?*

WAYS TO USE THIS BOOK

The book is structured with thirty lists. At the end of each list, there is a section called "Taking the Next Step." This is your opportunity to take simple steps to the marriage you want. These steps may include answering questions, self-evaluation, or simple steps to make changes. There are several ways you can use this book to improve your marriage.

Go day by day and repeat. Consistency over time equals impact. The best way to form habits to love well is by committing each day to the thoughts, attitudes, and activities at hand. The lists in this book are easy to read and comprehend. Focus on one each day. Study it, take some time to meditate on it, and apply what you have learned. Don't be overwhelmed. Take small bites. When you have completed the book the first time, start over and go another thirty days. It will reinforce everything you have learned, and you can choose a different task to focus on from the month before. For example, if it is the seventh day of the month you can focus on one thing from List 7 that your wife would like most. You can then make notes on your wife's reaction and on your progress. If a month later you have mastered that item you can choose another task from List 7 to work on for the next month.

Some of the action points are not easy to live out, and change does not happen overnight. But little by little, absorbing the truths laid out in this book will bring you closer and closer to the marriage you want.

Skip around. You may have specific challenges in your marriage that you know need work. Before skipping right to those things, we recommend that you begin with List 1. This will lay the groundwork for much of the book. Then go to the specific lists in the table of contents in need of attention in your marriage. You may want to camp out on a certain subject for a significant amount of time before moving on. Some of the concepts in this book, while simple to understand, represent a profound foundational shift that may require an investment of time and energy. Take as much time as you need.

Discuss it with your wife. Involve your wife in what you are processing. There is a counterpart to this book for her called *Lists to Love By for Busy Wives*. It contains content that is unique to wives, but it also includes some of the same principles and exercises as this book.

Each list will have questions and subjects to discuss with her. The whole purpose of this book is for you to learn how to love her and connect on a deeper level. Her perspective and input are richly essential. Listen to it and value it. Treat her opinion like holy ground. If there is one thing I would like you to learn faster than I did is that the purpose of this book is not to change your wife, as I tried to, but to change yourself and increase your active love of her.

LISTS TO LOVE BY
FOR BUSY HUSBANDS

LIST 1

7 Truths About Marriage

We both grew up on the coast of Florida and did quite a bit of boating. We threw a lot of anchors from the bow. Because the ocean floor in our area is very sandy, it was really important that the anchor was firmly secure. When a boat is effectively anchored it will stay in the same area. The wind, waves, and current will attempt to move it, but it will never travel far before the attached rope holds it from wandering. Anchoring takes more than just throwing the heavy item into the water. It takes focus and technique. A captain needs to be sure that the anchor has grabbed the sea floor, otherwise the boat will potentially drift off, running the risk of grounding or crashing into reefs or rocks.

So before we get into the rest of our lists, we must first be firmly grounded in truth. There are certain principles that are important to hold tight to so we do not drift off into dangerous places. There are seven truths that we have come to know that keep us grounded. They become particularly important when we experience rough patches in our relationship.

Truth 1. Marriage is not a quick sprint; it's a lifelong marathon.

A marathon is a long-distance race covering over twenty-six miles. Anyone who has run one will tell you it takes intense training, commitment, discipline, growth, endurance, and resolve. Marriage is the same way. There are attitudes and personality traits that will need training. There are relational muscles that need strengthening. And, most important, it is essential that both a husband and wife enter the marital race to go the distance and finish well.

Truth 2. Marriage is not a fifty-fifty partnership; it's a 100%-100%, give-it-all-you've-got relationship.

All too often, we've heard others say, "Marriage is a fifty-fifty partnership." But that's not true. When we excuse ourselves from putting one hundred percent into the relationship, we will constantly be comparing our efforts against our spouse's and questioning who does more in the relationship. In such a scenario, husbands and wives may even find themselves keeping a marital scorecard of who spends more, disciplines more, does the dishes more, cleans more or works more. Marriage is a 100%-100%, give-it-all-you've-got relationship. Marriage takes total commitment. You can't hold anything back. Day in and day out, you have to leave it all on the field.

Truth 3. Marriage is not always a stroll in the park; it's hard work.

Marriage is not easy. A good marriage requires hard work and "heart work." Like most other things in life, when we really work on our marriage, it only gets better and better. And when we really invest our time and energy into our relationship, more often than not, heart transformation occurs as well, which then brings a man and a woman into a more intimate union.

Truth 4. Marriage is not just about two people; it's about two people becoming one flesh.

Our deep desire in marriage is to know and be known, physically, emotionally, and spiritually. Marriage is about a man and a woman connecting and sharing on all these levels; two separate lives that come together and form one life. A man and a woman unite and set one direction and vision for their life together. They share in each other's pains and triumphs.

They share one another's bodies fully with each other. In no other relationship does God call for this type of physical union other than in a husband-and-wife relationship.

Truth 5. Marriage is not just "for better," it's also "for worse."

The most obvious moment of awe in a wedding is when the bride enters, and everyone stands and looks at her. She is glowing. She is striking. Her smile lights up the sanctuary. Awe is also in the face of the groom, who admires and desires her like no other can. The couple then recites their vows, which often include a promise to love one another "for better or worse." But on that day, few brides and grooms are thinking about the "worse" part...they can't imagine there ever being any speed bumps in life or in the relationship. The true character and depth of your committed love for your wife will not be shown in the best of times, but in the worst. Getting through difficult times while staying dedicated to each other shows the power of commitment.

Truth 6. Marriage is not just about happiness; it's about holiness.

Marriage is a holy union between God, a husband, and a wife—a union established to glorify God. God uses marriage to mold and shape us more into His likeness. He exposes our selfishness, refines our attitudes, and builds our character so we may be a better reflection of God. As author John Piper says, "Marriage exists to magnify the truth and worth and beauty and greatness of God."

Truth 7. Marriage is not about getting from your wife; it's about giving to your wife.

Focusing on ourselves will only produce misery. We are called by God to love and sacrifice for our wives. Marriage is about giving over getting.

TAKING THE NEXT STEP

- On a scale of 1 to 5, where would you rate yourself in your marriage with regard to each truth, with 1 being "Tired and Despairing" and 5 being "Energized and Hopeful"?

- Truth 1. Running the Marathon: Marriage is a long-distance race that requires intense training, commitment, discipline, growth, endurance, and resolve.

  1   2   3   4   5 ·

- Truth 2. Giving 100%: Marriage is a 100%-100%, give-it-all-you've-got relationship. Marriage takes total commitment.

  1   2   3   4   5

- Truth 3. Working Hard: A good marriage requires hard work and "heart work."

  1   2   3   4   5

- Truth 4. Becoming One: Two separate lives come together and form one life physically and spiritually.

  1   2   3   4   5

- Truth 5. For Worse: Marriage is not just "for better," it's also "for worse."

  1   2   3   4   5

- Truth 6. Holiness: God uses marriage to mold and shape us more into His likeness.

  1   2   3   4   5

- Truth 7. Giving over Getting: Marriage is not about getting from your wife; it's about giving to your wife.

  1   2   3   4   5

- Where in your marriage are you tired and where are you energized?

  _____

  _____

- Which truth is most important to you in your marriage right now?

  _____

  _____

- Ask your wife: Which of these truths is most important to you right now? Why?

  _____

  _____

~~~

3 Things to Remember About Marriage

Every year the most ambitious climbers head to the base of Mount Everest to conquer the world's tallest peak. The mountain sits just over twenty-nine thousand feet, as high as a typical commercial airline flies. When a person reaches over twenty-six thousand feet they are said to be in "the Death Zone," so-called because at that altitude, the human body can survive for only a short time, since it cannot acclimate to the harsh conditions. Most people bring supplemental oxygen with them, but that supply eventually runs out if they are up there too long.

Some climbers are so focused on reaching the summit that they forget it is only half the journey. They still have to hike *down* the mountain. It is at this crucial point that the amount of time at the higher altitude combined with a lower amount of oxygen to the brain can cause bad decisions, sometimes decisions that even cost them their lives. The real goal of the journey is not only getting to the top but also getting down safely. The best mountaineers have strict rules that they remember and adhere to, because they understand this goal. When these are forgotten they run into trouble.

Many people enter marriage thinking solely about the short-term gains or the peaks of marriage. They think about their own personal happiness. They don't consider the entire journey and what it will take to make it last a lifetime. While happiness may be a part of the marriage, making it the overall goal invites danger. Just as the best mountaineers need to remember and stick to certain principles to survive high on the mountain, the best husbands need to do the same in marriage. In order to have a full, lifelong marriage with your wife, you need to remember and apply the following principles.

1. Remember your vows.

"To have and to hold, from this day forward, for better, for worse, for richer, for poorer, in sickness and in health, to love and to cherish 'til death do us part." The day you and your wife were married was the day you promised all these things as you stood before God, before your family, and before your friends. Remember, this commitment you made was meant to be lifelong, and calling it quits would break that unconditional promise you once made with all your heart.

2. Remember what marriage is.

Marriage was never meant to be a contract to be broken, but a covenant to be cherished. Here is the clear difference between a covenant and a contract.

Covenant	Contract
Based on unconditional love between God, a husband, and a wife	Based on conditional consideration between two people
Sacrificial Action (i.e., I'll do it no matter what you do)	Reciprocal Transaction (e.g., If you do this, then and only then will I do that)
Based on Mutual Commitment	Based on Mutual Distrust
Seeks to Give	Seeks to Get
For Life	For Now

In a nutshell, a contract is all about what you get. A covenant is all about what you give.

3. Remember the purpose of marriage.

In my early years of marriage, I felt that an important part of Susan's "duty" as my wife was to make me happy. I was a bit more focused on me than on us. I didn't think so at the time, but now, looking back, I realize I relied on Susan to lift me up when I was down, to help me upon command, and to meet my physical needs when called upon...just to name a few.

Did you ever think, "Once I get married, *then* I'll finally be happy"? It doesn't take much experience in marriage to discover that this simply isn't true. The only person who can ever provide ultimate joy for you is God, *not* your wife. Perhaps realizing this truth means changing your expectations of her. Remember from the seven truths in List 1, marriage is not ultimately about happiness, but about holiness. It's a holy union between God, a husband, and a wife—a union established to glorify God.

TAKING THE NEXT STEP

- What was your favorite memory from your wedding day? Why? Ask your wife the same question.

  _____

  _____

- Based on how well you have lovingly followed through on your vows, grade yourself (A through F). Then have your wife grade herself.

You	*Your Wife*
____For better, for worse.	____For better, for worse.
____For richer, for poorer.	____For richer, for poorer.
____In sickness and in health.	____In sickness and in health.
____To love and to cherish.	____To love and to cherish.
____'Til death do you part.	____'Til death do you part.

- What vow will you commit to work on starting today?

  _____

  _____

  _____

LIST 3

~~

5 Powerful Words for Your Marriage

When God created the earth, He spoke it into being. He used words. Words are powerful and lasting. Using critical or hurtful words is like putting asbestos into the air. Airborne asbestos contains little needles that can be harmful, even fatal, when too much is taken into the lungs. I can all too easily recall hurtful things that have been said about me and that I've said to Susan and others. You can probably do the same. Words have the power to poison and even kill relationships.

On the other hand, words can also be used like pure oxygen that provides energy and life. Just as we know words can tear down, it's time to understand how powerfully words can also build a person up. Why not start building up your wife? Commit yourself to these five types of words, and you will breathe life into your marriage.

1. Respectful words.

After years of being married, it's easy to become comfortable with one another. But sometimes that comfort can turn into a lack of respect when you are no longer careful with what comes out of your mouth. Choosing to speak respectfully to your wife, and about your wife, means choosing words that will honor her, not undermine her. It also means choosing words that affirm her judgment and abilities, like "I really respect the decision you made."

2. Affirming words.

We can tell you from experience that our need for affirmation doesn't disappear with age. We both still desire to be validated by one another—and we desire that validation often. Cherish your wife by saying things like "You did a great job coaching our child on how to handle that issue" or "I was so impressed by the leadership you showed at work today."

3. Caring words.

It's easy to choose to dismiss your wife's need to talk about her day or what's going on in her life. We'd rather check Twitter, Facebook, or Instagram, send an e-mail, focus on the kids, or just relax. But we encourage you to sit down and give your full attention to your wife when she needs someone to turn to. Speak caring words to her in a moment when she is weak and needs to know someone is still on her side. "I'm so sorry to hear that…" or "Tell me more about how you are feeling" are caring words that will inject life into your relationship.

4. Encouraging words.

Truett Cathy, the founder of Chick-fil-A, once asked me, "Mark, how do you know if someone needs encouragement?" I said, "I don't know, Truett, how?" He responded, "If they are breathing!" Everyone needs to hear words of encouragement, especially our wives. So let's encourage them to press on when they are down. Let's inspire them with our words.

5. Appreciative words.

Finally, it's important to speak words of appreciation to your wife. No one wants to feel taken for granted. Keep your eyes open for ways to express appreciation to her. "Thank you for doing the laundry" or "I'm so grateful for your help on that project" are the types of words that will uplift her and show your appreciation to her.

TAKING THE NEXT STEP

- List in order the two types of words that are most important to your wife. Then ask your wife which ones are most important to her and compare your answers.

You	*Your Wife*
1. _____	1. _____
2._____	2._____

- What is one type that you need to focus more on? Concentrate today on using the type of words you need to focus on. For example, if it is appreciative words, then write down one or two appreciative things you can say to your wife and say them. Take note of your wife's response.

_____

_____

_____

_____

_____

LIST 4

7 Things Husbands Should Stop Doing

One day I came home from work to find Susan and one of our teenage daughters arguing. I stood listening for a few moments and then thought I would intervene to end it. I then proceeded to address each of them individually on what they were doing wrong and why they each should stop. In essence, I spoke to each of them as if they were children. I put Susan on the same level as our child.

Later that evening Susan brought up the incident. She told me in no uncertain terms that she felt unsupported. I had undermined her authority rather than back her up. She felt as if I wasn't on her team. Challenging the way she was handling the situation, if necessary, should have been done in private. It was something I needed to stop doing. There have been many bad habits like this in my marriage that have taken hard work to stop.

As I began to think about this I came across a good article written by Dave Boehi, author and senior editor at FamilyLife, called "40 Things Husbands Should Stop Doing." I picked some from his list, came up with some of my own, and added my own thoughts on each.

1. Stop dishonoring your wife by criticizing her in front of your children or others.

You may think you're being clever or funny, but it's not helpful to your marriage or honorable to your wife to criticize her, especially in front of others. Your kids need to see you modeling how to be supportive and complimentary, not critical, of your wife.

2. Stop comparing your wife to other women.

Saying something like "Why can't you be more like Karen?" is demeaning and devaluing to your wife. She is created with immeasurable value and worth. Cherish and honor your wife for who she is, not for what she does or doesn't do.

3. When your wife tells you about a problem she's having, don't immediately try to fix it.

She may just need you to listen to her. It's in our nature as men to want to fix things. So when Susan tells me about something, instead of jumping in to fix it, I often ask her something like "Do you want me just to listen or do you want my input on how to deal with it?"

4. Stop trying to control your wife.

As I mentioned in the Introduction, this one has been a struggle for me, especially in the early years of our marriage. I thought Susan should think, behave, and do things just like me. I soon learned not only to accept our differences, but to cherish them. I let go of the reins and let Susan be the woman, wife, and mother God created her to be.

5. Stop being passive in disciplining and training your kids.

Parenting is a team effort and is not just Mom's job. Be actively involved with your wife in disciplining your children and in training them up to walk in truth and love.

6. Don't be alone with any woman who is not your wife or a family member.

Susan and our team at Family First, our national nonprofit organization, know that I've always had a personal policy not to travel with, have lunch, or meet with any other woman alone. To do otherwise would only invite temptation into my life.

7. Stop feeding your sexual desires from any source other than your wife.

Whether it's flirting with another woman or looking at pornography, avoid anything that could take your mind, heart, or body away from your wife. Treat your sexual relationship with your wife as something to be protected, not just enjoyed.

TAKING THE NEXT STEP

- The things you need to stop doing may be ingrained habits. Making changes can be challenging. As I shared in the Introduction, early in our marriage, I was often critical of Susan. It became an unpleasant habit. I had to commit to changing my behavior. So, go back and star the top thing you need to stop doing. Then commit to stop. To ensure that the habit is broken, you may want to ask someone to hold you accountable.

LIST 5

3 Keys to Unlock the Door to Intimacy

Imagine you're on the *Family Feud* television show. The show host steps up to you and your opponent and says: "We asked one hundred people this question, and the top three answers are on the board. What are the keys to intimacy in a marriage?" I can imagine a lot of words that might race through your mind. *Sexual compatibility. Time. Romance. Open Communication. Sexual compatibility. Compromise. Forgiveness. Kindness. And sexual compatibility!*

All of those are good answers. But I'd like to suggest that there's a strong case to be made that *trust* is the door to emotional and physical intimacy in marriage. It is an essential ingredient in becoming one.

Sometimes trust needs to be restored from a wrongdoing. If so, the wrong needs to be admitted, and the admission should be accompanied by a sincere request for forgiveness followed by the granting of forgiveness by the offended mate.

You may be thinking you haven't done anything wrong. That's the wrong way to think. We all make mistakes in our words, in our thoughts, in our actions.

Whether building trust or restoring it, trust is not something that anyone owes you. Trust must be earned. That means that you need to provide something to your wife in order for her to trust you. It is not something you do just one time but consistently, day in and day out, over a period of time.

If trust is the door to intimacy, then there are three keys to opening that door. In order to trust you, your wife must have complete confidence in the following from this day forward.

1. You are who you say you are.

Your wife needs to know that everything about you is real. Whether you are with your family, friends, or coworkers, your wife needs to see that you are the same person wherever you are and whoever you are with. She needs to see you living a consistent life. Your wife needs to know that you are rock solid, not a person whose personality or behavior is constantly shifting. Consistency is key!

Also, when you and your wife got married, you promised to be there for each other "for better, for worse, for richer, for poorer, in sickness and in health...'til death do us part." You also committed to become "one flesh." That means the other person should be able to rely upon those promises— that you will not tear the marriage apart and that you will be there, as her husband, no matter what happens.

2. You will always speak the truth.

There are no such things as "little white lies" or "half truths." What you say is either true or it is not. Let me illustrate. If your wife asks you something simple, like "What have you been doing?" don't just say, "Mowing the lawn." If you have also been watching television and checking e-mails, say so. Remember: Truth is the whole truth. To build trust, speak truth in everything, big and small. Doing so will help build your wife's confidence in your trustworthiness.

Speaking truth also means not keeping secrets from her. Whether it's a purchase you made, an addiction you have, an illness you're experiencing, or a place where you've been, nothing should be kept from your wife. Keeping fun surprises may be an exception. Sharing challenges, problems, and your emotions with your wife may be difficult initially, but will help build trust and, ultimately, intimacy in your relationship.

3. You will always do what you say you'll do.

In simple terms, when you say you'll do something, the other person can *check it off the list* or *take it to the bank*. It's a *done deal*. If for some reason you are unable to do it, let the other person know immediately. Also, the seeds of suspicion and distrust seem to germinate when the person working to rebuild the trust does unpredictable things. For example, if you are going to be unusually late coming home from work, tell your wife and let her know why.

As you rebuild trust in your relationship, remember that one of the best things you can do is to ask your wife, "What can I do to earn your trust once again?" Then be sure to listen carefully and take action.

TAKING THE NEXT STEP

- In what ways are you different around friends and coworkers than you are around your family?

  _____

  _____

- Is there any time in your life when you speak so-called half truths or embellish?

  _____

  _____

- Make a list of the promises you made this week. Did you follow through? If not, why?

  Promise

1. _____ Kept? _____ Yes _____ No

   Why?_____

2. _____ Kept? _____ Yes _____ No

   Why?_____

3. _____ Kept? _____ Yes _____ No

   Why?_____

LIST 6

5 Unfair Expectations You May Have of Your Wife

The first year of marriage can bring a lot of pitfalls. Both people bring into the marriage ideas about how things are supposed to be. A friend recently told us a story about a friend of his whose wife made him dinner a few days after they were married. After dinner he kicked back and began to relax, as did his wife. That's when he turned to her and said, "Aren't you going to do the dishes? My mom would have had all of the dishes cleaned up by now." It was a very unwise thing to think, and an even more unwise thing to say. Fortunately he had quick reflexes and dodged the vase that was thrown at his head!

Whether our preconceived notions come from the way we were raised or TV and movies, they have a way of causing us to set some unfair expectations of our wives. Unfair expectations create a barrier to intimacy and a growing relationship. Here are five common examples.

1. Expect that she always needs your help.

Many of us have known the pain and frustration of a micromanaging boss. This is the boss that assumes you don't know what you're doing or that you're probably doing it wrong. Husbands can do the very same thing to their wives, and it hurts. What you may assume as being helpful, she may see as a lack of trust or an assumption of weakness.

2. Expect that she never needs your help.

It's amazing how often the words *always* and *never* are associated with unreal expectations. Yes, we just said that a husband shouldn't expect that his wife always needs help, but it's also unfair to expect that she never needs help. Whatever the issue or task, it's best to ask your wife first whether or not she needs your help, and, if so, how you can best help her.

3. Expect that she's always ready for sex.

Generally, women don't think about sex as often as men do, but husbands are apt to forget this. A man compounds the problem when he views his wife like a video game... expecting that with a few pushes of the right buttons, she'll be turned on by him instantaneously. Men, we all need to be reminded that sexual intimacy is not just mechanical; it is emotional and even spiritual.

4. Expect that she will agree with you on financial matters.

Financial issues are one of the biggest sources of marital conflict. Husbands may assume that it is their responsibility and that they'll make all the financial decisions. We grew up in homes like that. Our dads handled the finances and generally handled them well, but our moms really weren't involved in those decisions. But a better way is for a husband to sit down with his wife and discuss things like how much debt, if any, they are willing to incur, what their spending priorities are, and how much they want to save and give to others. In our marriage, we work closely together on financial matters and neither one of us moves forward on any major purchase or gift without consulting with the other.

5. Expect that she should always know you love her.

As the joke goes, "I told you I loved you when we got married... if anything changes, I'll let you know!" It's not fair for you to assume she knows you love her. Wives need to hear it from their husbands, see it in their actions, and feel it in their interactions with them. And through those married years, a wife wants to know that her husband still finds her attractive.

TAKING THE NEXT STEP

- What are some of the unreal expectations you've had of your wife? Can't think of any? Ask her.

  _____

  _____

- Today, do this: Ask your wife if you can help her with something and tell her you love her. If you win points, do it again. In my house it helps with number 3.

LIST 7

10 Things Wives Want to Hear from Their Husbands

In the movie *The Family Man*, Nicolas Cage plays a man named Jack who chooses not to marry his college sweetheart Kate, instead opting to pursue his career. The movie picks up years later where Jack has become a Wall Street tycoon, one of the richest and most eligible bachelors in New York. Everything changes when an angel gives him a glimpse of what his life would have looked like had he chosen to marry Kate. He is disappointed to find out that he is a tire salesman from New Jersey with a messy house and two young kids.

Eventually he becomes enchanted with the kids and has a revelation about Kate. At one point he looks at her and says, "Wow. All these years I've never stopped loving you." She replies, "That's all I wanted to hear." There are certain things a husband can say to his wife that are like the correct puzzle piece fitting in her heart. Here are ten things your wife wants to hear from you.

1. "Thanks for all you do for our family."

Yes, you work hard. You may even feel that your load is a million times heavier than your wife's. But your wife works hard, too...and a little thanks goes a long way.

2. "You are a great mom and wife."

If you really want to make her day, go beyond saying "thank you" and praise her for doing a good job.

3. "Let me do that for you."

Your wife realizes you are exhausted when you get home from work. She probably is, too. So offer to help out. Start with something small, like cleaning up after dinner. Or, if you really want to score points, do the laundry or something else you normally don't do.

4. "I love you so much."

Did you notice the extra words after "I love you"? Telling your wife you love her is a great start, but telling her *why* you love her, how *much* you love her, or that you'll love her forever will melt her heart.

5. "You are beautiful."

No matter her age, her size, or how long you've been married, a woman loves to hear that you think she's attractive. Don't just say, "You look nice." Instead, use adjectives like *great, lovely, fantastic.*

6. "Let me watch the kids."

If you already spend time each day with your children and watch them on your own regularly, good job! If you don't, think of it this way: When you offer to take care of the children, your wife gets to recharge her batteries. A wife with a recharged battery is usually more patient, kind, and loving.

7. "Let's go out tonight."

Take charge of your next date night. Plan it out on your own. This shows your wife that you enjoy spending time with her.

8. "I'm sorry you had a hard/frustrating/ disappointing day."

These words let your wife know that you are aware of and care about what's going on in her life.

9. "I would marry you all over again."

In one sentence you're telling your wife you value your life together and that you're committed to her.

10. "How can I be a better husband to you?"

Hearing these words will either make your wife burst into tears, smile like a kid in a candy store, or, if she's completely shocked, laugh uncontrollably. Before you ask this question, though, be ready to hear what she has to say without being defensive.

TAKING THE NEXT STEP

- Star the list items you say. Circle the items you don't say. Ask your wife which are the most important to her, write them down, and focus on those.

  _____

  _____

- What are other things your wife wants to hear from you? Add to the list here.

  _____

  _____

LIST 8

5 Things Wives Wish Husbands Knew

Susan has a highly creative and energetic personality. Her mind is constantly moving and thinking of ideas. As I've stated before, our personalities are very different. When we had kids, she went from a career woman to a stay-at-home mom. Around that time we also started the organization Family First. She was happy to be involved in planning and executing events. However, she also was heavily involved in many other things. She was all over the place and constantly moving. I couldn't understand it, and I tried to rein her in by changing her.

The truth was that she was overcommitted and needed to give her time and energy to fewer things. But what I didn't know at the time was that she needed a creative outlet and had so much energy that she needed to apply it somewhere.

Eventually she would say, multiple times in fact, "You just don't get me." In my effort to change her and rid her life of these outlets, I was crushing her spirit. Now that I know this about her, I am able to love her better by encouraging her to do the things that bring her life.

I wish I had known that earlier in our marriage and I know Susan does, too. It would have saved us both some pain. As I was thinking about these things, I asked Susan and several other women generally what things wives wish husbands knew. Here are the results.

1. Wives desire appreciation.

Sometimes, it seems like wives are the hardest-working people on the planet. But do we tell them? It is our privilege to be the recipient of much of their work, and it is our job to thank them for all the things they do—whether it's making dinner, cleaning the house, or working hard to support our family. Expressing your appreciation will encourage and motivate her in a big way. Bottom line: Don't ever take her for granted. Be her biggest fan.

2. Wives desire attention.

When you get home from a long day at work, don't always go straight for the TV or your phone. Ask your wife about her day and then tell her what your day was like. Listen with empathy, and don't make light of what she's saying. The first ten minutes when you walk in the door set the tone for the evening. By giving her your full attention, it shows that you truly respect and care for her.

3. Wives desire affection.

All women crave affection, no matter how long they've been married. They want to hold your hand, to be told they're beautiful, and to be kissed tenderly. My wife has flat-out asked me to be gentle. My bear hug works only occasionally. She wants tender affection. Because ultimately, physical affection reinforces that you're still in love with her even after years of marriage together.

4. Wives desire patience.

After getting input from some of the married ladies in the office, I found out that I am not the only husband who struggles with being impatient. Over the years, I've been learning how to practice patience and will continue to work on this virtue for the rest of my life. Men, I encourage you to talk calmly and patiently through issues with your wife. If you don't, you will be in constant conflict; or worse, she may even shut down. When a disagreement escalates, you may want to agree to reconvene later after you both cool off.

5. Wives desire friendship.

Your wife desires a companion—someone to turn to when frustrating circumstances arise at work or when the kids are out of control. It's important to be a man who will listen to her, share her difficulties, and then comfort and help see her through the trials. By the way, friendship goes both ways. Your wife also wants you to trust her with your thoughts, feelings, and challenges in life.

TAKING THE NEXT STEP

- What does your wife desire most—appreciation, attention, affection, patience, or friendship?

  _____

  _____

- How do you plan to meet that need today?

  _____

  _____

LIST 9

11 Things a Husband and Wife Must Agree On

A few years ago, our house flooded in a storm. The flood was so bad that we had to completely gut our house and take it down to the studs. As our contractor started the reconstruction, he checked the foundation and found some problems. There were some cracks and deterioration in the pillars that were holding the house up. My contractor explained to me that if we didn't shore up the foundation, we'd start having some real problems with our house. We could do all the framing, drywall, and painting and make the place look nice, but if we didn't make sure the foundation was sound, we'd always struggle to have a sound structure.

The same holds true in marriage. Husbands and wives need to make sure their marital foundation is sturdy by agreeing on certain concrete principles. If they don't, it's only a matter of time before their relationship will start to sink, and maybe even collapse.

When we started to date, Susan made it clear that praying together was foundational. I had my own time of regular prayer and often prayed with my friends, but I didn't think praying with the girl I was dating was a big deal at that time, so I didn't make it a priority. Well, it was a big deal to Susan. So much so that she didn't feel like we could move forward in our relationship without praying together. After a short break in our dating relationship, during which I seriously thought about the importance of us praying together, I felt convicted and shared with Susan that we did need to pray with one another. Shortly thereafter, we got engaged. The foundation for our lifelong marriage had been established.

Here are eleven concrete things a husband and wife must agree on.

1. **You are married for life. Therefore, divorce should never be considered, except possibly for unfaithfulness, abuse, or abandonment; and even then only after seeking wise counsel and applying God's word to your situation.**

2. **Your marriage is a top priority, and you will do whatever you need to do to strengthen it.**

3. You will strive to meet the sexual needs of your mate. Sex will not be withheld as punishment or because of lack of interest.

4. You will always be honest with your wife and will speak the truth in love. That means no secrets.

5. You must agree on whether or not you would like to have children.

6. You must agree on when and how you will discipline your children.

7. You must agree under what moral code or belief system you will raise your kids.

8. You and your wife will always honor your parents, but you and your wife—not your parents or in-laws—will make the decisions in your marriage and for your children.

9. You must agree on how much you will spend, save, and share.

10. You must agree on where you will worship.

11. You must agree on your career priorities: Whose career outside the home will become the focus?

TAKING THE NEXT STEP

- Choose the three items that are most important to you. Have your wife do the same. How many overlap?

  _____

  _____

- If you disagree on a point, what can you do to fully understand your wife and see things from her perspective?

  _____

  _____

LIST 10

9 Keys to Understanding What Your Wife Is Really Saying

Yes, we both speak English. But after twenty-seven years of marriage, I've determined that Susan, and most other women, have a double secret female code that they completely understand, but we men don't.

I've determined that it's time to decode it. In order to do so, I've confidentially spoken with several female informants who have helped me to decipher just some of their secret code. Those informants have asked to remain anonymous out of fear that other wives will shun them for disclosing what has remained a mystery for all these years.

So for all the men out there who thought it was impossible to understand women, here is a key for decoding your wife's words.

1. **"I'm fine" means** *I'm not fine, but I'm not ready to talk about it.*

This is a classic line that most husbands have heard. The instant you hear it, you know that everything is certainly *not* fine. And even though you may want to work it out right away, sometimes it's best to just give her some time and space. Be sure to let your wife know that you're sorry if you hurt her feelings in some way and that you're ready to talk when she is.

2. **"Didn't you go out with your friends last weekend?" means** *I know for a fact that you went out with your buddies last Friday night, and I want to spend time with you this weekend.*

Your wife is very aware of how you spend your time. And where you invest your time is one important sign of what you value. She wants to be valued and cherished. So sure, spend time with your friends, but let her know she's always number one.

3. **"How was your day?" means** *I want to reconnect with you.*

Most couples don't spend all day, every day together. There are jobs and kids and things to be taken care of. So when your wife asks about your day when you get home, this is her way of trying to reconnect after being in different worlds. Instead of a one-word answer, give her a story or two that will make her feel close to you again.

4. "What are you doing today?" means *I've got some things that I want you to do.*

It's Saturday morning and your wife asks the question, "So what are you doing today?" What she's saying to you is: *If you don't have any really important plans, don't make any because I've got a lengthy honey-do list that you need to get done.*

5. "Do you need some help with that?" means *I want to be a part of your team.*

For an example, let's take the time you were trying to fix the TV. In the midst of the tangle of cords and your growing frustration, your wife asks if she can help. You immediately assume she must be questioning your abilities and doubting your skills. But she may simply be trying to love you well by offering her help. So rather than push her away, let your wife support you with what you're doing.

6. "Let's talk about this some more" means *I don't agree, but I want to understand and support you.*

Life is full of decisions—from small, daily ones to huge, life-changing ones. A big part of marriage is being able to make choices together with your wife. So when your wife wants to discuss a decision, it's important to recognize that she isn't automatically disagreeing. Her intention is to be wise and find a compromise that you can both agree on.

7. "We should go out this weekend" means *I want you to take initiative and make the plans.*

I can't put enough emphasis on the importance of continuing to date your wife all through your marriage. While some couples have a weekly date night, we have found that a date every other week was more realistic when our kids were growing up. So when your wife mentions the coming weekend, this is an intentionally planned comment. She is trying to give you a clue that she wants to feel special and loved by going out with you. So take the hint and plan something romantic for the two of you.

8. "Is there something you're forgetting?" means *There's definitely something you're forgetting.*

Your wife knows there are certain days when you have a busy schedule ahead of you and are more apt to overlook things. So when your wife specifically asks if you're forgetting anything, the answer is most often a big "Yes!" Whether it's your lunch on the counter or a good-bye kiss for her, be sure to stop and pay attention when your wife mentions this.

9. "You don't have to get me anything for my birthday" means *I do want something, but I want you to put time and energy into picking it out.*

The important thing to realize is that all thoughtfulness and specialness is taken away the moment your wife has to tell you what to get her for her birthday. Instead, a gift is a great way to show her how well you know her and love her. So put some thought and energy into giving your wife a present she won't forget. If you have no idea what to get, try asking one of her friends.

While there is so much more to decode, I hope this helps you to better understand your wife and love her well. And, by the way, please don't let her know that you know some of the secret code.

TAKING THE NEXT STEP

- What do you think your wife says often while actually meaning something else? Are any of them on this list?

  _____

  _____

- Think about the ways that you communicate. Are you straightforward and clear? In other words, are there things that you say that your wife needs to decode?

  _____

  _____

- If you were graded (A through F) on listening and understanding your wife, what grade would you get?

  _____

  _____

~

4 Ways to Break Free from the Pornography Trap

There are some beautiful beaches in the world that have hidden dangers. When water floods sand below the surface, the sand particles get pushed apart. The result is a muddy mixture of the two that can't support the weight of a person. When someone walks over it, they sink down. It's a trap known as quicksand. As the person sinks down, his body pushes out the water, creating a vacuum effect that secures its victim tighter and tighter. Sometimes it takes only moments to absorb someone into a desperate situation.

This is what pornography does to millions every day. It starts simple enough without any sign of danger: a movie on cable or the click of the mouse. A man tells himself there's nothing wrong with it, or perhaps that it's not that bad, even though he keeps it secret. Pretty soon what started as "controllable" and "here and there" turns into a habit, and he sinks deeper and deeper. It's a trap that binds its victim, with seemingly no way out.

It's an addiction that squelches intimacy. Intimacy takes an investment of time and energy, while pornography is a way to manufacture cheap, fleeting thrills instantaneously. Those manufactured feelings begin to replace actual intimacy with a spouse, even when a couple watches it together. Meanwhile it makes a wife feel insecure and betrayed. It's time to escape the pornography trap. Here are a few ways to do so.

1. Face it and own it.

You need to admit your porn watching to someone. We encourage you to share your struggle with your wife if she doesn't know, even if it causes pain and hurt feelings. Perhaps speak to a trusted friend, counselor, or pastor first so that you can prepare and pray. Secrets keep us enslaved. When secrets are brought into the light of day, the ugliness is exposed. Face it and own it. This is the first step toward being free.

2. Break the cycle.

Research shows that when porn is viewed, neuro-transmitters called dopamine flood the brain (similar to heroin use). These dopamine releases give us the feeling of pleasure. When the doses are too high, as is the case with habitual porn viewing, the brain adjusts to restore balance by reducing the amount of dopamine available. This causes a decreasing amount of pleasure experienced. So a person needs to consume larger amounts of porn and potentially more graphic images to receive the pleasure he had before. Lower dopamine levels can make a person feel depressed, causing him to go back to porn to stimulate more. It is a cycle. The good news is that when a person quits watching porn, the brain readjusts and corrects its dopamine levels. It's simply a matter of breaking the cycle by not feeding the appetite. When it's not fed, the appetite will decline in time.

3. Find group support and encouragement.

You can't do this alone. The great news is that you're not alone. Find a group of like-minded people that you can meet with regularly and be completely honest. Make sure it is a group that is high on accountability and encouragement. Find people that will be real with you and pray with you about it. Perform an online search of porn addiction support groups, or seek out churches with programs in your area. Another alternative is counseling, which can be done one-on-one or preferably in conjunction with a support group. They can give specific coping techniques when the urges come calling, act as another level of accountability, and uncover unseen triggers.

4. Make the choice for more.

In my book *All Pro Dad: Seven Essentials to Be a Hero to Your Kids*, I shared that Howard Wasdin, a former navy sniper and SEAL Team Six member, discussed what it takes to be a part of an elite force. He said this: "Mental toughness. I can take just about anyone and make them physically strong. A lot of people showed up at [training] who were much more physically capable than I was, football players and athletes in phenomenal shape, and they were the first to quit. Mental toughness is a must to make it through training, much less through combat." You can do this. You can quit pornography, but it will require mental toughness and a conscious choice to escape the trap.

The key to a full life is found in relationships. Porn alienates people from one another and causes relational difficulty. It trains the brain to live in a fantasy world rather than connect with a real human being. Selfishness is nurtured, because porn is instant gratification at the expense of other people becoming dehumanized. That leads to guilt, loneliness, and isolation. It is a short-term exhilaration with a long-term lower quality of life. Intimacy takes effort, patience, and investment, but the reward is abundance. Relational intimacy refines selflessness and the ability to love. Quitting porn is a choice for more. Commit to that choice every morning, every hour, and every evening.

TAKING THE NEXT STEP

- Do you look at pornography? Do you believe it is OK?

  _____

  _____

- Does anyone know? Does your wife or anyone know about your present and past with porn? If not, tell someone and develop accountability.

  _____

  _____

LIST 12

7 Reasons Your Married Sex Life Lacks Passion

When you got married, you didn't imagine this was how it would be. After all, you love each other. You are attracted to one another and have good chemistry. However, when you are intimate, there is something missing. Maybe it is a new development in your relationship. Maybe the busyness of life, indifference, or even bitterness have created a chasm in your marriage. Or, perhaps it has always been that way and you hoped it would eventually change, but it hasn't. Your married sex life is passionless.

Sex is not always going to be earth-shattering. But when it consistently lacks passion over time, it can become divisive. The frequency of its occurrence tends to become less and less. Filled with unsatisfied desires, some turn to unhealthy things such as porn or an affair to attempt to quench their thirst. In order to find the solution, it is important to identify the underlying problem. If your married sex life lacks passion, it could be because of one of these reasons.

1. Inhibitions.

When a husband or wife is inhibited, it normally comes from a negative view of sex. This negative view may have formed from something as dramatic as abuse. Others may have had parents who, with very honorable intentions, tried to dissuade them from having unmarried sex by communicating that all sex is bad. That association sometimes remains even after marriage. Feelings of guilt, fear, and self-consciousness come rushing in, as if they are still doing something wrong. Unfortunately, these are normally deeply engrained (particularly abuse) and the person may need counseling to move toward healing.

2. Lack of prioritizing and initiative.

Sex is not set as a priority. Energy is given to everything else: raising kids, pursuing careers, or maybe even pursuing other people. This normally happens when one person puts sex low on the list, leaving the other frustrated. Picking up on the frustration of their spouse, they do it out of obligation. Nothing takes the passion out of physical intimacy more than when a husband feels like his wife has sex with him as a favor or vice versa. Both husband and wife need to keep it high on the list of priorities.

3. Hidden bitterness.

When unresolved issues and a lack of forgiveness linger below the surface, they create disunity. Passionate sex is fueled by the level of connection a couple is experiencing. Undealt-with hurt will turn the heart into a petri dish of bitterness. The relationship electricity will dim until it eventually shuts off.

4. Lack of honesty.

Whether it is for fear of either rejection or hurting the other person, a lack of honesty will place limits on the sexual relationship in a marriage. It shows a lack of trust. It's important to be able to communicate what each person finds enjoyable and what they don't. This doesn't mean all desires need to be met, but that there should be a safe environment for free and open dialogue. One of the beautiful things about physical intimacy is knowing things about one another that no one else knows.

5. Focus on performance.

The focus of sex should be to love, connect, and enjoy one another. People can become preoccupied with performing, because it makes them feel more adequate or even powerful. It's good to tune in to your wife and work to meet her desires as long as the motivation is one of giving. When the motivation becomes performing, then it becomes self-serving and breeds disconnection.

6. Loss of attractiveness.

This can be physical, but in most cases it is deeper. Maybe it is the abrasive or disrespectful way she treats him that causes him to view her as less attractive. It could be that he has no initiative in life or with his family. That lack of initiative turns her off. For example, he may have become a couch potato or content in a life that lacks any kind of personal growth. On the other hand, the attractiveness of her husband may increase for her if he planned adventures for the family and continually challenged himself personally and professionally. Address the issues honestly but with kindness and gentleness.

7. Familiarity.

Both of you are caught in a cycle of doing the same routine. It's gotten predictable and boring. A couple can easily fall into this trap, but it's important to change things up and perhaps even try something new that you both are comfortable with.

TAKING THE NEXT STEP

- Which of these do you and your wife struggle with?

  _____

  _____

- When you think about these, do any seem to be a risk to your sex life?

  _____

  _____

- What about your wife turns you on? Does she know?

  _____

  _____

- Rate the Passion of Your Sexual Intimacy:

- Touching

  Low 1   2   3   4   5   **High**

- Kissing

  Low 1   2   3   4   5   **High**

- Talking

  Low 1   2   3   4   5   **High**

- Frequency

  Low 1   2   3   4   5   **High**

- Variety

  Low 1   2   3   4   5   **High**

- Buildup

  Low 1   2   3   4   5   **High**

- Attractiveness

  Low 1   2   3   4   5   **High**

- Have your wife rate the above as well and discuss together.
- Ask your wife: What things do you want me to do more when we are making love? What are things you don't like?

_____

_____

LIST 13

4 Decisions That Define Forgiveness

Ed Thomas is a hero in his community. For thirty-six years he was a high school football coach in a small town in Iowa. He held high standards of decency for himself, his family, and his players. When a tornado destroyed much of the town, he led the cleanup and rebuilding effort. The next spring Coach Thomas was in a makeshift weight room when one of his former players, Mark Becker, who recently had been diagnosed with paranoid schizophrenia, came in and shot him multiple times. Becker's father was captain of Ed Thomas's first team, and his younger brother was a part of the current team. Both the Thomas family and the Becker family were devastated. The Beckers weren't sure if they would be able to continue to live in that community. Those fears were quickly relieved.

Immediately after the murder, the Thomas family, publicly and privately, reached out to the Becker family to offer prayers and forgiveness. Their loving act set the tone for the community and followed the example set by their husband and father.

When you are wronged by someone you have a choice. You can choose to hold on to the hurt and spend the rest of your life with the pain, bitterness, and anger. Or you can choose to be released from it, healed, and freed. It's a decision to forgive the person who has hurt you.

So let's talk about what forgiveness really is. When you really forgive someone, you are making a decision to release, embrace, pardon, and grow.

1. A decision to release.

In the process of forgiving, the first barrier you have to remove is within your own mind. You must make the decision: *I will not dwell on this incident.* Don't replay the incident in your mind. We realize that is easy to say but hard to do. When that reel begins to play in your mind, intentionally push the Stop button. Realize that it will not make things better. Dwell on what is good and ask God to give you the strength to withstand the onslaught of those attacks on your mind. When you forgive, you are also proactively choosing to release your bitterness, resentment, vengeance, and anger toward the person who has hurt you.

2. A decision to embrace.

When you truly forgive, you are intentionally embracing mercy and grace. Putting it simply, mercy is not giving someone what they deserve. Grace is giving someone what they don't deserve. Why show mercy and grace to this person who has deeply hurt you? For two reasons: First, God extends his perfect mercy and grace to you. And He showers His perfect love upon you...every time, all the time. Second, remember the Golden Rule? It basically says, "Treat others as you want to be treated." So when you make a bad mistake, when you hurt someone, when you wrong someone, how do you want to be treated?

3. A decision to pardon.

Merriam-Webster's Learner's Dictionary defines *pardon* as "an act of officially saying that someone who was judged to be guilty of a crime will be allowed to go free and will not be punished." I remember from my days of practicing law that once someone is pardoned or acquitted in a court of law, they cannot be tried again for the same offense. That's called double jeopardy. So when you choose to pardon your offender by forgiving them, you are letting go of your right to punish them for the offense in the future. You are basically saying, *I will not bring this incident up again and use it against you*. In so doing, you are choosing to hold on to the person, not the offense.

In our twenty-seven years of marriage, we have forgiven each other for various offenses and hurts in our relationship—or at least we thought we had. There have been occasions where one of us has brought up a past offense the other thought was pardoned, only to find that court was still in session on the issue. Real forgiveness must involve a complete pardon.

4. A decision to grow.

When you forgive, you are taking away the power the wrongdoing wields over you and using that power toward your growth, perhaps the growth of your relationship. You are making the statement: *I will not allow this matter to stand between us or hinder our personal relationship*. Think of forgiveness as something that will change your life—by bringing you peace, emotional and spiritual healing, and hope—and, hopefully, the life of the one you have forgiven.

TAKING THE NEXT STEP

* What is a situation where you needed to be forgiven?

  _____

  _____

* What is the hardest thing you have forgiven your wife for? How did you feel afterward? What were the results?

  _____

  _____

* Is there anyone whom you need to forgive today?

  _____

  _____

* Is there anything for which you need to ask for forgiveness?

  _____

  _____

LIST 14

10 Texts to Send Your Wife in the Next Ten Days

It's difficult to remember the world before cell phones. Unless you were one of the few people with a car phone, you couldn't check in with anyone. If you were picking someone up from the airport or meeting someone, it needed to be well coordinated. You could call someone only if they had a phone at home, at the workplace, or the building where they happened to be at the time.

One of the most important ways Susan feels loved is through words of affirmation. So in those earlier days, I used to leave little yellow sticky notes on the bathroom mirror, the car steering wheel, or the refrigerator telling her how much I loved her. I would still recommend doing that, even in a world of smartphones. But texting (unless you're driving, of course) can be a great way to send a much-needed note to the most important person in your life.

I encourage you to take a challenge. Send ten texts to your wife in the next ten days that express what she means to you. You can think of your own, or here are ten to help you.

1. Of all the guys in all the world, I'm honored to be the one who gets to do life with you.

2. Today's been a rough day, but thinking of you makes it all worth it.

3. You're my best reason to go to bed at night and my best reason to get up in the morning. Can't wait to see you later today!

4. No matter how you feel about yourself today, remember this: There's at least one person on this earth who knows how awesome you are—me!

5. What can I do to make your day or night easier? Give me some tips...I want to help.

6. I may not always understand you, but I'm trying because I love you. Thanks for being patient with me.

7. I admire your ability to _____. That is so important to our family. Just wanted you to know that.

8. Remember when we started this life together? Even if we knew then what we know now...I'd do it all over again.

9. If I could drop what I'm doing right now to be with you, I'd do it in a heartbeat. Love you!

10. I just wanted to hit the Pause button at work today to let you know how grateful I am to be your husband.

TAKING THE NEXT STEP

- This can be an easy experiment. Start texting today, either one or several a day. What kind of response did your wife have with each text? Which did she seem to like the best?

  _____

  _____

LIST 15

7 Things Your Wife Should Expect You to Be

After we got married, we discovered our differing gifts and divvied up household responsibilities according to those gifts. For example, Susan is the financial person, so she pays the bills. I can fix things—well, some things. When something is broken, I'm expected to repair it, or at least try to repair it.

While personalities, responsibilities, and many other things will differ from marriage to marriage, there are non-negotiable marriage expectations that should be the same for all husbands. So here are seven things your wife should expect you to be. Remember: Each is a way in which you demonstrate your love for her.

1. Trustworthy.

You need to be authentic...the real deal. We talked about building trust in List 5. It means you will always speak the truth and never keep secrets from your wife. Susan knows I don't keep secrets from her. I'm always "open for inspection." She knows my computer password and can access it any time to see what I am reading and looking at. She can also see my calendar at any time. Susan can also pick up my smartphone any time to read my texts and e-mails and check out what kind of music I'm listening to.

Being trustworthy also means that you'll do what you say you'll do. If you tell her you'll pick up some milk on the way home, make a note to remind yourself to do it. Don't forget and dismiss it as not being important.

2. Faithful.

You're certain you'd never give yourself physically to another woman...but what about mentally and emotionally? Even if you don't go looking for porn, do you let your eyes and thoughts wander when something or someone alluring comes into view? Just for a moment or two? One key to remaining faithful to your wife is to keep completely away from temptation. That means not sharing your emotions or marital struggles with another woman. And it means not traveling or dining alone with the opposite sex.

3. Provider.

In our homes, we have a clear responsibility to provide for the physical needs of our wives and children. That means that we must work and earn money to provide for those needs. That doesn't necessarily mean we have to be the sole breadwinner. Many couples both have jobs outside the home. If that's so, where and how are we helping in other areas of home life?

By the way, don't think that putting a paycheck on the counter covers it all either. In addition to financial and physical needs, we must also support our family emotionally and spiritually.

4. Protector.

Chivalry may not be dead, but it's in poor health. For me, the growing lack of gentlemanliness in society is a concern. Opening a door for a woman is a sign of respect. Keeping to the street side of the sidewalk when you walk with her is a manly mark of protection.

We live in a dangerous world: Someone is sexually assaulted every 107 seconds. Your wife and your children need to feel safe and protected—and not just physically. You may have a home security system to guard against burglars. But what about other kinds of home invasion, like harmful media? Are you on the alert for your wife and family?

5. Leader.

Some people get a bit bent out of shape over this one, but a man is called to lead his family. A man who loves his family well will lead his family well. When a man's wife and children know that he always has their best interests at heart, they'll follow him. Love is leadership's unseen essential.

6. Servant.

This is the antidote to the previous leader thing getting out of whack. As leaders, we should not look to be served but to serve in our homes. What does that look like in your home? How are you serving your wife and children? What are you doing to ensure that they are becoming all they can?

Being a servant means that the world does not revolve around you. That her needs and desires, their needs and desires, take precedence over your planned fishing trip, your golf game, or your night out with your buddies. When they know they are important and a top priority, they will follow you.

7. Sexually intimate.

It's easy to think that sexual intimacy is only a priority for guys. But it's important for women, too, though perhaps in a slightly different way. Women derive physical pleasure, too, of course, but there is also a big emotional component. Your pursuit demonstrates that she is desired and delighted in, that she is still the one. It is also an active expression of your faithfulness. So don't look at your neighbors' lawn. Instead, take the time to water your own grass, so that it's the greenest it can be.

TAKING THE NEXT STEP

- How well are you meeting these expectations? Give yourself a report card in each subject (grades A to F). And then have your wife grade you.

Your Grading	*Your Wife's Grading*
____Trustworthy	____Trustworthy
____Faithful	____Faithful
____Provider	____Provider
____Protector	____Protector
____Leader	____Leader
____Servant	____Servant
____Sexually Intimate	____Sexually Intimate

- Where do you need to improve and why?

  _____

  _____

LIST 16

~~~~

8 Expectations for a Great Marriage

The first major battle for the United States in the Vietnam War was known as the Battle of Ia Drang. The American forces in that battle were commanded by Lt. Col. Hal Moore. Surrounded and facing overwhelming odds, Moore and his soldiers withstood the onslaught for a week. One of the things Moore credits as a reason for that success was the love and devotion the soldiers had for one another. However, equally as important was Moore's consistent studying of the battlefield and knowledge of his enemy. He knew their strategies and the angles they would take to attack. Knowing what to expect enabled him to position his forces in places that gave the greatest chance of victory.

In marriage, it is important to have love and devotion for one another. However, it is also important to know what to expect. So, here are some things you should expect in marriage. Now some of them may sound negative, but they aren't meant to be. We just need to be prepared for the challenges that are likely to arise so that we can combat them effectively. Here are eight expectations you'll encounter in marriage.

1. Expect conflict.

Conflict will happen, and that's okay, *if* you handle conflict in a loving, mature way.

2. Expect delays.

Planning for your future is a great thing to do as a couple, just understand that things don't always arrive on schedule—not babies, not raises, not the sitter.

3. Expect disappointments.

File this in the "you're both only human" category: As hard as your wife may try, she will never be perfect. She will fall short of your expectations at some point; and if your expectation of her is to make your world perfect, she won't be able to do that. She also won't be a mind reader, nor will she anticipate all your needs. Don't let your disappointment dull your passion for her.

4. Expect to be annoyed.

What was once appealing is now annoying. Be ready for that habit of hers you found so adorable while you were dating, to become annoying. But remember this, there are things you're doing that are likely annoying your wife, too. Cut her some slack and continually focus on her good qualities. If you just can't overlook what's bothering you, talk about it in a loving, kind way.

5. Expect to think you're doing more.

You might feel like you're doing more dishes, more laundry, more bedtime reading with the kids, more yard work, more taking the garbage out. You get the idea. When you start feeling put out and put upon, take some time to assess the situation. Then, instead of attacking your wife and demanding more help, sit down and calmly express your desire to do your jobs well, and ask for help.

6. Expect to disagree with some of your wife's decisions.

Just because you are one in marriage doesn't mean you will agree on everything. And, guess what? That's okay. Respect her right to have a different opinion than you. Don't shoot down ideas automatically. There is often more than one way to get the job done.

7. Expect not to be attracted to your wife.

This may never happen to you. You may go through your entire marriage being passionately attracted to your wife. But if, at some point, you're just not that into her, pray that you will have a loving heart and stoke the embers so your fire will burn bright once again.

8. Expect to be with your wife until the end.

This is a mental safety net. Even when you're furious or extremely disappointed with your wife, you will not think of leaving. You can't, remember? You're with her until the end. This expectation also helps you realize that you should work to make your marriage the best it can be, because you are in it for the long haul.

TAKING THE NEXT STEP

- Which of these expectations has been the biggest challenge in your marriage?

  _____

  _____

- Which of these do you feel like you can begin to address today, and what will you do? For example, if you get frustrated and annoyed when you come home to a mess (which I often did when our children were young), start expecting the mess on the ride home from work. Make a plan of how you are going to react before you walk through the door. Instead of getting upset, change your clothes, gather the kids, and make cleaning up a game. Make it fun for the family.

  _____

  _____

LIST 17

9 Things You Should Never Say to Your Wife

In September 1991 the fishing boat *Andrea Gail* left the port of Gloucester, Massachusetts, heading toward the Grand Banks. Tragically, it would never return. It is a story told in the best-selling book and movie *The Perfect Storm*.

After over a month of sword fishing, the ice machine of the *Andrea Gail*, which kept the catch fresh, malfunctioned. They decided to head back to port, but they received a warning of a growing storm blocking their path home. It was a hurricane. With over a decade of experience, Capt. Billy Tyne steered the *Andrea Gail* directly into the storm. It was a fatal error. What he could not have anticipated was how intense the storm would be. Hurricane Grace had collided with a nor'easter coming off the coast. When the two merged, it produced one of the most powerful storms in history. The angry and ferocious sea would sadly overtake the boat and its crew.

In chapter 3 of the book of James, God gives us this warning, "Take ships as an example. Although they are so large and are driven by strong winds, they are steered by a very small rudder wherever the pilot wants to go. Likewise, the tongue is a small part of the body, but it makes great boasts." The words we use direct us where we want to go. This is especially true in relationships. When we choose words that have empathy or encourage our wives, it brings connection. However, when we speak harshly, we steer our relationship directly into the storm. When it's done with consistency, the storm can sink the marriage.

How can you avoid these storms? It starts by controlling the rudder and identifying things a husband should never say to his wife. We surveyed a number of wives to tell us one thing they do not want to hear from their husbands. Here are the top responses.

1. "Calm down. Relax!"

Several variations on this theme, like "Chill out," made the point loud and clear. When our wives are upset about something, these phrases are not helpful. This can come across as making light of their stress and the issues that cause it.

2. "What's wrong now?"

Words like this—or, worse yet, like "What's wrong with you?"—strike a nerve because they treat our wives like they are a problem to fix or a machine to control. These phrases lack empathy and also risk demeaning our wives or the situations that concern them.

3. "What were you thinking?"

There's a theme here. The ladies are trying to tell us something, men. Sometimes the words we use sound more appropriate for a prosecuting attorney or a kindergarten teacher. This phrase is belittling. It only serves to convey the assumption that very little thought, or good thought, went into her decision. It certainly does not build her up.

4. "What did you do all day?"

Here's yet another example of how assumptions and ignorance can lead to disrespect and pain. When we say these condescending words, particularly to a mom who works full time taking care of the kids, we show how little regard we have for their contributions inside and outside the home—especially compared to what we do.

5. "Is it that time of the month?"

I probably don't need to explain this one too much. Men, whether it is "that time of the month" or not, I would encourage you not to say it.

6. "I don't love you anymore."

Saying something like this pierces the heart of a woman and will not be forgotten. Remember—love is not just a feeling, it's a decision. Choose to love your wife for life.

7. "Are you going to eat all that?"

Ouch. When you say that, you're basically telling your wife she is fat. Not a good idea.

8. "Get off my back...you're always nagging me."

Whether she's nagging you or not, saying this is not going to make things better. The better course of action would be to sit down with her and explain, in a kind way, how the things she says bother you and how they make you feel.

9. "You're just like your mom!"

This is usually said in a derogatory way. When said, you're not only insulting her but also her mom and your mother-in-law. Let's guard our tongues with our wives as much as we guard our money, time, and other resources. What we speak can do so much good, but in only a few short words, we can do so much harm. Let's use our words to build up, not tear down.

TAKING THE NEXT STEP

- Have you ever used one or more of these phrases? If so, which one caused the most damage?

  _____

  _____

- What other phrases have you discovered that cause more hurt than help in your marriage?

  _____

  _____

- When your wife is upset, what are the phrases or attitudes that tend to soothe and bring peace to her?

  _____

  _____

7 Things You Should Stop Doing to Your Wife in Public

We were at a barbecue with a number of families. Hosting a lot of people at your house can be very stressful. The host couple at this barbecue was definitely feeling the stress as they ran around trying to serve all their guests. The husband was manning the grill and asked his wife to bring him something. I guess she didn't bring him what he wanted, because he snapped in a loud voice, "Really?! This is *not* what I wanted! For once can you bring me what I ask for?!" We felt bad for her as she ran back into the house, flustered, to try and get exactly what her husband wanted.

He shouldn't have been speaking to her like that to begin with, but the fact that it was in public made it even worse. I must confess that I am not innocent. There have plenty of times where I have been critical of Susan in public and it hurt her. Perhaps you are doing things *in public* that are harming your wife and hurting your marriage. If you are doing any of the following, it is time to make a change.

1. Stop criticizing your wife to others.

Being critical of your wife hurts her reputation. It damages whatever respect others have for you, too. And it conveys that your marriage is not a safe place for your wife to be herself.

2. Stop making your wife the punch line.

This behavior belittles her and suggests that you don't care, even if you do. At some point, your wife and others have to wonder, *Are the jokes really jokes?*

3. Stop sharing the details of your love life.

At social functions, we've all too often heard other men talk very negatively about their sexual relationships, or lack thereof, with their wives. When they do so, they are really breaching trust with their wives. Intimacy is built on trust. When you expose your private love life in your marriage, especially in a derogatory fashion, to public scrutiny, you can easily destroy trust.

4. Stop treating your wife like a child.

We've also heard men in public instructing and ordering their wives around as if they were children. It's humiliating.

5. Stop checking out women who aren't your wife.

You may have heard someone say, "I can look at the menu as long as I don't order." That's wrong thinking. Your wandering eyes and careless words may cause your wife to feel insecure, inadequate, and without value. It's degrading to her as well.

6. Stop constantly correcting and contradicting your wife.

When your wife is telling a story, stop interrupting to inject missing parts or correct mistakes. It demeans her. Instead, look for opportunities to honor your wife and help her save face in public. Be her hero.

7. Stop trying to impress other women.

Whether it is with your looks, abilities, or success, there is only one woman you should be trying to impress. Our culture does not value modesty, and when you flaunt your attributes, it appears you're advertising yourself or are available to others. Act like you're only available to one person: your wife. Because that's the only person you should be available to.

TAKING THE NEXT STEP

- Put a checkmark next to any of these you have done in public.

____ Criticize her

____ Make her the punch line

____ Share intimate details

____ Treat her like a child

____ Check out other women

____ Correct and contradict her

____ Try to impress other women

- How does it affect your wife? How does it affect her when you do the opposite?

  _____

  _____

- Why do you think you do any of the above?

  _____

  _____

- Ask your wife: What is one thing you wish I would change about the way I talk about you to others?

LIST 19

5 Ways to Woo Your Wife to the Bedroom

Remember when you and your wife were newly married? It was really difficult to keep your hands off each other. You wanted her and she wanted you. That felt so good. It was awesome. There's no better feeling than being desired. After a few years of marriage, and particularly after having kids, things have a way of changing. You are still ready to go almost every night, but she's not. What happened? You feel like you don't have sex as often anymore, and when you do, it may feel like she's doing you a favor.

You work out, you look good, but it doesn't make a difference. You're lost. This whole married-sex thing was supposed to be different. So, what should you do? Part of it involves understanding her perspective and focusing on these five things. But remember, you can't do these for one day and expect immediate results. You need to commit to these things without looking for anything in return, because they are ways to love her. That is the overall goal. However, when they are done with consistency they are likely to lead to you and your wife having physical intimacy more often.

1. Talk to her about her.

Find out how she is feeling—her insecurities, fears, and struggles. Ask her questions like, "So how does that make you feel?" Or say, "Tell me more about that." And then actively listen. Also share how you are feeling. Look at her— no distractions. Get tunnel vision on her. While we feel more connected to our wives by having sex, our wives need to feel connected beforehand. You may have talked with her about daily logistics or superficial things. She needs more. She wants to be seen, heard, and known. The feeling of disconnection causes her loneliness. It's like she's trapped in a dungeon alone. You need to free her.

2. Affirm her.

She needs to feel your passion for her in your words, body language, and eyes. Tell her she's sexy and why—particularly when she makes a negative comment about herself. When you get home from work, greet her with a long hug and kiss before you greet the kids. Look into her eyes, and don't be in a hurry to look away. When you're out, direct your eyes at her rather than other places. Give her a look that communicates, in a room full of people, she's the only one you want to talk to.

If she's given birth, her body has changed. She knows it and she probably thinks about it all the time, constantly comparing herself to other women. Even when she returns to her pre-kid body, I guarantee she's still comparing— desperate for affirmation. The best place she can get it is from you.

3. Be patient with her.

Reach out to her with physical and emotional tenderness. That's what she wants and needs. Try to meet her needs before your own.

Studies show that over the course of a relationship, a woman's desire for sex decreases while her desire for tenderness increases. The problem is that our desire for sex often stays just as high as always. Even at its highest state, her appetite might not have been as high as yours and may never be. Recognize this reality and keep initiating, but be tender.

4. Give her some rest.

Being physically intimate is difficult for a woman when she is feeling tired, stressed, or depressed. Run some errands for her, clean the house, or do the dishes. If she is stressed or depressed, rub her shoulders without her asking you. Give her a foot or full body massage. Tell her to kick back and relax. Give her music to listen to and light some candles. Take her tension away. If she is a mom, take the kids out for a day. But all these things need to be done without expecting any immediate payoff. The idea is to wow her first. The woo will come later, after you wow.

5. Talk to her about how you feel.

Make sure you are not prosecuting or pressuring her. Encourage her about how amazing she is as a wife. Let her know, though, that you miss her, want her, and desire her. Your biggest concern should be for more intimacy—a significant need for each of you.

TAKING THE NEXT STEP

- On a scale of 1 to 10, how ready is your wife for intimacy?

  _____

  _____

- If she is below a 5, which of the above suggestions can you begin working on today? And how many days do you think it will take to reconnect with her? For example, if Susan has been pressed at work, busy meeting the needs of our children, and taking care of her dad, I know that giving her some rest and relieving her workload is one of the best things I can do.

  _____

  _____

- How many times a week do you think it is healthy for you and your wife to be physically intimate? Ask your wife what she thinks and compare answers. It may sound rather unspontaneous, but we have five kids, and finding time without scheduling is challenging, so we have one standing appointment every week. If it happens more, it is a bonus.

  _____

  _____

5 Common Mistakes Men Make in Marriage

When I was in high school, I played football. A consistent routine every week was watching game film. Whether we won or lost a game, we always watched what we did so that we could correct our mistakes. The camera doesn't lie. Everything we did well and the things we did poorly were right there on the screen for everyone to evaluate and provide feedback. There were times when the feedback from coaches would be direct and feel harsh. But I appreciated knowing the things that needed correcting so I could improve week after week.

Imagine if you were shown game film of all of your interactions with your wife. What mistakes do you think you would find that need correcting? Are there any mistakes you make over and over again? Many of the mistakes you make are probably some of the same mistakes I, and other men, make. Now, I know some of you are thinking about the mistakes she is also making, and I understand. However, you cannot control her. You can only control what you do.

Here are five common mistakes men make in marriage and what you can do about it.

1. They don't think of the needs of their wife.

You schedule a date night with your wife. Good job! However, you wait until you are walking out of the door to say, "What do you feel like doing?" Don't do it. Plan ahead. Make a reservation at your wife's favorite restaurant. Call the babysitter yourself. You will get an A for effort!

2. They don't listen.

Being a good listener is something I've struggled with for a long time. I'm a bottom-line kind of guy, so the fewer the words to make a point, the better. But over our twenty-seven years of marriage, Susan has taught me how to be a better listener, although she would tell you I've got a long way to go.

Here are a few things I've learned about listening: Don't assume you know what your wife is going to say. Don't tune her out because you have heard it all before. Do keep eye contact at all times. Do ask her questions like, "So how did that make you feel?" Do empathize with her by saying things like, "I'm so sorry you had such a rough day, honey." Listening to her will bring you closer and, as we discussed in List 19, it can increase physical intimacy as well.

3. They don't understand their wife.

If we're having a discussion about something, and Susan is on a roll about her feelings and thoughts on the subject, I might think it's enough to nod my head and throw an occasional "Mm-hmm" into the mix. But what's even more important to her is that I demonstrate a genuine curiosity about her, wanting to understand her even if I don't agree with her. The goal of listening is understanding.

One way to do this with your wife: Repeat back what you think you heard her say and what you think it means. Ask her sincerely, without sarcasm or anger, "Is this what you're saying? Help me to understand you better."

4. They don't know their wife.

Do you remember getting to know your wife when you were dating? When was the last time you just spent time talking *with* her, not *to* her? Ask what her dreams are, where she would like to go on vacation, or what good book she has read lately. Here are some more questions for you to ask her to help you:

What would your dream house look like?

If you could travel anywhere, where would you go?

What day of your life would you like to live over again?

Which married couple do you admire most?

What is your favorite activity that we do together?

5. They don't confide in their wife.

Your wife wants to be included in your entire world. Confide in her—your dreams, your work, your life. Be vulnerable. Many men try to hide their insecurities or true feelings from their wives for fear of appearing weak or possibly causing friction. If work is stressful or causing you to worry, then let her know. Tell her the things you want to do in your lifetime. Let her know what you want your marriage to look like in the future. Give her full access to who you are, the good and the bad. Your marriage bond will only be strengthened.

TAKING THE NEXT STEP

- Discover one new thing about your wife today—a need, desire, or dream.

  _____

  _____

- What will you plan or do to delight your wife this week?

  _____

  _____

LIST 21

8 Creative Ways to Flirt with Your Wife

Remember senior class notables in high school? Most Athletic, Most Witty, Most School Spirit, Best All-Around, and Most Likely to Succeed were just a few of them. Well, I'm a bit embarrassed to tell you that they created a new category for me...Most Flirtatious!

Now, that's not necessarily something to be proud of, but I am proud that I still like to flirt with my wife, Susan. Married people should flirt with each other...a lot!

Flirting, by definition, is playfully communicating sexual interest or attraction to someone. And flirting with your wife can reap lots of benefits. Flirting can communicate, yet again, that you still find your wife attractive and vice versa. It can create more intimacy with your wife. Flirting in front of your kids, even though they may react with something like "That's gross," will reinforce a sense of love and stability at home as they see their parents showing a healthy desire to be with each other.

So here are eight playful, fun, and creative ways to flirt with your wife.

1. Leave a note for her (maybe on her pillow or the bathroom mirror) before you go on a trip.

"I can't wait to get back to see you!" may be something you'd like to say. Or, let her know you appreciate something specific about her, like "Thanks for taking care of so many details when I'm gone...you do a great job!"

2. Leave a note on her car's rearview mirror saying, "I'm jealous of this mirror because it's looking at you."

3. Serve her practically in a surprising way.

If you don't normally cook, make her favorite meal and have a candlelight dinner...just the two of you. For some wives, it's the simple acts of service that lets her know you love her.

4. Text her when you get up and when you go to bed to let her know she's the first person on your mind and she's your last thought of the day.

I texted my wife, Susan, saying "You are awesome! I love you!" before we went to sleep even though she was right next to me in bed. I loved how it made her feel, and it surprised me just how much it mattered to her.

5. Come up with something corny, but fun, to tell her or to e-mail her.

Like "You must be overdue from the library because you've got FINE written all over you!" Or, "Can I have a fry to go with that shake?" (Search the Internet sometime for more lame or goofy ideas!)

6. Turn on your favorite song on your smartphone and dance in the kitchen with her when she least expects it.

7. Get dressed up, go outside, knock on the door, and ask her out for a date.

The kids will really get a kick out of this one.

8. Post a sincere, unexpected comment of praise for her on Facebook or Twitter.

This has to be done in a humble way and should have substance to it. Don't showboat, but do let the world know why she means so much to you.

There are many ways you can show your wife you still dig her after all these years. Find what works for you, because not every idea that we shared here is going to work for you. One final thought: Even if your kids act grossed out, you're not only showing them you are into their mom, but you're also setting their expectations for how to be a healthy, flirtatious spouse someday.

TAKING THE NEXT STEP

- Whatever you did with your wife when you first started dating worked, because she married you. Think back: In what ways would you flirt with her? In what ways would she flirt with you?

  _____

  _____

- Flirt with your wife today. Do what you used to do or try some of the suggestions above. If you have kids, have fun with it and enjoy grossing them out!

LIST 22

7 Things You Must Know About Your Wife

As I mentioned in List 19, "5 Ways to Woo Your Wife to the Bedroom," I learned early that if Susan was tired and stressed out, physical intimacy was probably not going to happen. So one Saturday, I started to strategize about how to leverage that concept, and somehow I rationalized that if I did more housework, I would get points. That Saturday, Susan was out having fun with some friends. I had all day in front of me and decided to do all of the laundry.

I was on it and couldn't wait for her to come home. She was not ten seconds in the door when I grabbed her to show her my mountain of fresh, clean, folded clothes. She said in an unenthusiastic tone, "Oh, thanks for doing the laundry." That was it. She then turned around and headed upstairs. I couldn't believe it. All my hard work and that was her reaction. Why? It just was not a big deal to her. Acts of service are not her love language, words of affirmation are. So then I knew that I needed to zero in on affirming her with my words.

How well do you really know your wife? I don't mean the color of her hair and her eyes, or where she was born and went to school. That's her biography, her exterior. But what about her inner life, her thoughts and feelings, her hopes and fears? Knowing the answers to these seven questions will help you understand and love her well. They will help you tune in to your wife.

1. What is her love language?

What means most to her: receiving gifts, quality time, words of affirmation, acts of service, or physical touch? If you have not yet read Gary Chapman's classic book, *The 5 Love Languages: The Secret to Love That Lasts*, you may want to. It's such a good resource and will help you identify the way she feels most loved.

2. What is her biggest fear?

We're not talking about being scared of heights or disliking going to the dentist, I mean the deeper, heart things that perhaps speak of her past: fear of abandonment or betrayal, or of not being a good-enough mom. How can your words and actions help address her concerns?

3. What spells romance for her?

Sometimes when I see a guy at the grocery checkout with a bunch of flowers and a box of chocolates, I can't help but wonder how much thought has really gone into the gesture, even though I've done that myself on occasion. Maybe they are her favorites, but it seems a bit cookie-cutter. How would your wife respond? Maybe she'd prefer you to hold a duster rather than a bouquet. We've heard of research that found women felt more amorous when their men did the housework. It's a reminder that a wife's emotional engines are finely tuned and need the right fuel.

4. What makes her feel valued?

Your wife needs to know that she is important for what she does, and for who she is. You might start by making a point of thanking her for her actions—and generous words spoken in front of others can be especially meaningful. But also be sure to invite her opinions, acknowledging you value her wisdom. And what small actions communicate to her that she is cherished? A simple touch on the arm each time you pass can speak volumes.

5. What does she enjoy doing?

We all have things that delight us, that recharge and energize our lives. Maybe if there are children in the house, it's just an uninterrupted morning alone in bed and a hot bath. Perhaps she loves thrift shopping or playing tennis with friends. It could simply be alone time with you, talking heart to heart, or even doing yard work together.

6. What makes her laugh?

Research has proved the old adage: *Laughter is the best medicine.* Exercising our funny bone is good for our health. But I have noticed that for many couples, the longer they are together, the less they laugh. Somehow the busyness and seriousness of life seem to take over. Whether it's your spontaneous silliness or a romantic comedy, find the thing that will lighten her spirits on a regular basis. You could start by discovering some fun online video clips, or just finding her tickle spot.

7. What does she struggle with most in your marriage?

This one may take the most courage to respond to, but chances are you know the answer, deep down. It's that area that maybe makes you anxious or defensive when she goes there. It could be financial struggles, parenting challenges, or feeling a lack of intimacy. Her insecurity may raise up in you some feelings of inadequacy, but don't turn away. Are you willing to step into her doubts and fears, to do what you can and must to help, to be strong with and for her?

TAKING THE NEXT STEP

- Test yourself about your wife. Answer these seven questions how you think your wife will answer. Then have her answer them. Check your answers. How many are a match?

	Your Answers	Her Answers
Love Language?	_____	_____
	_____	_____
Biggest Fear?	_____	_____
	_____	_____
Romance?	_____	_____
	_____	_____
Feeling Valued?	_____	_____
	_____	_____
Enjoys Doing?	_____	_____
	_____	_____
Makes Laugh?	_____	_____
	_____	_____
Biggest Struggle?	_____	_____
	_____	_____

- Did any of her answers surprise you?

  _____

  _____

- How often do you spend time creating space so she can do her favorite thing? What is something you can sacrifice to make sure she is able to do it?

  _____

  _____

6 Things to Do When You're Lonely in Marriage

As humans, we are not meant to be isolated. We all crave deep and lasting connections with other people. But we know it's possible to feel alone in the middle of a crowd, and it's possible to sleep in the same bed with a spouse for years and still feel lonely. Many of us never expect to be lonely in marriage, hoping that our wife will be the lifelong companion who saves us from loneliness. Over time, however, couples can gradually disconnect from one another and find themselves feeling isolated and withdrawn.

Loneliness is not just about physical proximity, it's about emotional connection. FamilyLife's Dr. Dennis Rainey and his wife, Barbara, explain: "You may have sex, but you don't have love. You may talk, but you don't communicate. You live together, but you don't share life." If you're feeling lonely in your marriage, here are some ways to reconnect with your wife.

1. Make the first move.

Feelings of loneliness are seldom felt by only one person in a relationship. If you're feeling isolated, chances are your wife is, too. Take the first step to reconnecting with her, even if it's just a small gesture. Open up to her about how you feel, and give her an opportunity to do the same. Healing cannot begin if you hide or mask your pain.

2. Forgive past hurts.

Especially if you have been feeling alone for a long time, hurts have likely been building up in your marriage. Nothing breeds loneliness more than unforgiven hurt and conflict. If you have been wronged, make the decision to forgive your wife. And if you have wounded her, seek her forgiveness immediately.

3. Spend time together.

This seems like a no-brainer, but sometimes couples get so busy or caught up in their individual lives that they neglect to simply spend time together. The less time a couple spends together, the more likely they are to feel distant from each other. This can be resolved by deliberately scheduling date nights in, date nights out, TV-free nights, and occasional weekend getaways—just for the two of you.

4. Make your time count.

The quantity of time together is really important, but so is the quality of that time. Couples have to be intentionally focused on their time together to create a marital connection. When you and your wife are talking, put down your cell phone, set aside distractions, and focus on each other. Find ways to bond over shared experiences: taking a walk, cooking dinner, going to a concert or sporting event, or playing a board game or cards together. Encourage and compliment your wife. Make your moments together count.

5. Prioritize physical closeness.

This is not just referring to sexual intimacy, though that is certainly an important part of marital closeness, but also to the little things that may have fallen by the wayside like holding hands or snuggling on the couch. The key to resurrecting physical touch is to start small. Sit close to each other, give neck massages, and pull out a surprise kiss.

Getting closer physically will naturally lead to feeling closer emotionally.

6. Don't be afraid to ask for help.

While the idea of seeking outside input for your marriage can be intimidating, nearly every couple can benefit from good marriage counseling. Getting an outside perspective can be extremely helpful to you and your wife.

You may feel lonely in your marriage, but you are not alone in the struggle for marital intimacy. We have all experienced loneliness in our lives, but you don't have to feel it in your marriage.

TAKING THE NEXT STEP

- Have you ever felt lonely in your marriage? If so, what have you done about it?

  _____

  _____

- What can you do to reconnect with your wife? Which one of the above suggestions will you commit to today?

  _____

  _____

LIST 24

∼⌒⌒

5 Ways to Use Body Language to Connect

For most of our marriage Susan has been the cook. She likes it. However, when all of the kids got older, went to college, and started their careers, she went back to work outside the home. So I started to dabble in self-taught culinary arts. Now that I know a little bit about cooking, I find myself looking over her shoulder and sometimes questioning what she is doing. In fact, the other day she was cooking while talking to our daughter and I didn't think she was paying enough attention, so I said, "Susan are you going to stir that? I don't want it getting burnt." Wrong move. She just turned and gave me "the look." Have you ever gotten "the look"? Although she didn't talk, I immediately understood what she was saying. The look expressed, *Oh really?! You're going to tell me how to cook?! You couldn't even make a sandwich until I taught you how to do it.* I received the message loud and clear.

Our nonverbals communicate just as much as our spoken words. In the case of Susan, it was easy to see, but many times it is subtle and takes a trained eye. Understanding body language will help you avoid breakdowns with your wife. Becoming an expert in postures, arm motions, and facial expressions can save hurt feelings and enhance communication in your marriage. Take a look at how you can use your body language to connect with your wife.

1. Use your eyes.

The eyes are a lamp to the soul. Making eye contact shows that you are engaged and interested. Looking away occasionally communicates that you are processing what she is saying. However if you look away, and off into the distance a lot, more than likely you are going to give her the impression that you are not paying attention. She'll feel as though you don't care. If either of you are looking at the ground, it means there are feelings of intimidation, defeat, hurt, or sadness. Rapid blinking denotes someone is feeling uncomfortable or upset. Squinted eyes can communicate sympathy, but more often send a message of skepticism. Eye rolling is a sarcastic dismissal and should be avoided at all costs.

2. Use your mouth.

Besides the obvious frown and smile, the mouth can reveal quite a bit. Pursed lips, for example, tell her that you either don't approve or trust her—or what she is saying. Biting the lips reveals anxiety or worry. Hands covering the mouth is someone that is hiding an emotional reaction. It may reveal some insecurity or lack of confidence.

3. Use your hands.

The hands can disarm and draw in, or they can push away and make her defensive. Keeping your hands open is inviting. It says that you are open-minded and ready to hear what she has to say. Never close your fist. It communicates anger and that you are closed off. Be careful when using exaggerated motions with your hand. Sometimes it shows excitement which can be good in certain situations, but in an argument it escalates the tension.

4. Use your posture.

When thinking about posture, one powerful way to connect is by mirroring. It's making the same pose and forming the same posture as her. Many times we do it naturally without thinking about it. Mirroring powerfully communicates a desire to connect and be on the same page. When you see her strike the same pose, it means you are on the right track. On your part, keep this in mind and consciously do it when you two are having trouble connecting. In a disagreement, stay away from slouching, crossing your arms, and putting your hands on your hips. If you are slouching, it may show that you have checked out. Crossing arms says that you are defensive and closed off. Hands on the hips means you are aggressively challenging her.

5. Use your vocal tones.

Be aware of your volume and pitch. Raising your volume escalates things and shows you are trying to dominate. Lowering your volume can communicate that you are trying to calm things down; however, going too low (close to a mumble) can give off the impression you are withholding or hiding something. A higher pitch shows excitement or irritation, while a lower pitch is more relaxed. During an argument, try to maintain a lower pitch to help defuse things. Be aware of how placing an emphasis on certain words can change the meaning of what you say. Emphasize words of love and understanding.

TAKING THE NEXT STEP

- How has your body language escalated a situation in the past? How has it helped defuse a situation?

  _____

  _____

- How can you change from using negative body language to using positive body language?

  _____

  _____

- When your wife communicates with you, do you feel like you understand her body language, or have you misread her before?

  _____

  _____

LIST 25

10 Ways to Affair-Proof Your Marriage

Maybe you know of someone who experienced infidelity in their marriage. Their spouse cheated and they really never saw it on their radar screen. Others experience the devastation of an affair and, if they paid attention to their relational radar screen, they may have seen it on the horizon. The reality is that you can often see it coming and you can sometimes prevent it from happening as well. Does *affair-proof* mean that if you do these 10 things that it's a 100 percent guarantee that you will never experience an affair? Of course not. It means that you are doing some very important things that will significantly decrease the likelihood of an affair striking your marriage.

Commit yourself to the following practices to affair-proof your marriage.

1. Establish guardrails.

With your spouse, identify those slippery areas that could spell danger for your marriage. For example, some people have jobs where they travel a lot. Guardrails are especially important when you are away from home.

Several years ago, I made a trip from Tampa to Orlando, Florida, for a business meeting. I arrived at my destination, and the guy I was meeting with came out to my car to greet me. He noticed that one of my office team members drove up in a separate car, and he said, "Oh, Jennifer must have another meeting today in Orlando, huh?" "No," I replied, "I just don't travel alone with a woman, other than my wife, of course." He seemed a bit surprised, but I think he understood my reasoning, even though we spent a few more dollars in gas to get there in two cars. I also avoid intimate conversations about my personal life with other women. Many affairs begin when people start talking about their personal pressures and problems with another person besides their spouse. They feel the other person empathizes and understands them better. This can then lead to a feeling of closeness, which, if left unchecked, can lead to an intimate emotional or physical relationship.

2. Stop viewing pornography.

As we discussed in List 11, "4 Ways to Break Free from the Pornography Trap," pornography destroys people and relationships. Porn creates unrealistic and false expectations for your sexual relationship with your wife. It promotes the lie that relationships are all about getting instead of giving. There's another lie people tell themselves about pornography: "I'll do it one more time, then I'll stop." But some is never enough. Pornography is like a drug; you always need more and more and something stronger and stronger for the high to continue. As a result, soft porn leads to hard porn. And pornography often leads to an extramarital affair. So, what should you do? Start by bringing to light what has been hidden in darkness by sharing your struggles with your wife, pastor, or friend. Immediately flee from it and avoid pornography completely. Put your computer in a very public place in your house or get rid of it for a season of time. Never erase your computer history. Allow your wife to hold you accountable and give her all of your passwords to your computer and cell phone.

3. Date your wife.

Establish a date night and treat this time as sacred by putting it in ink on your calendar. Again, as we shared in

List 10, some people are able to do this every week. You may find that works for you. We find that every other week seems to work better for our schedules. Make your date something fun and interactive. Have dinner at a new restaurant, play tennis, go bowling, go dancing, take a walk, or take a class together.

4. Fire up the romance.

The best way to avoid a spark with someone else is to keep the home fires burning. It doesn't take much to start the romance. A short love letter only takes a few minutes to write. Putting a sticky note on the mirror telling your wife that you can't wait for your date tonight can work wonders. These small gestures show your wife that you've thought of her and will help you reinforce your commitment to your spouse.

5. Be affectionate.

Being playfully affectionate with your wife will also stoke the home fire and will help snuff out any hint of an outside spark. Here are a few things I like to do to show affection to Susan: wink at her across the dinner table; give her big hugs; hold her hand when we're on a date; and cuddle in bed… without always expecting number 6 on this list.

6. Enjoy physical intimacy often.

It happens all too often, one spouse starts exploring a sexual relationship outside the home because that desire is not being satisfied in his marriage. As we shared in List 19, "5 Ways to Woo Your Wife to the Bedroom," exhaustion, busyness, emotional distance, and many other things cause sexual encounters to wither. While those may be valid reasons, they must be dealt with to the extent possible so that the opportunity for frequent physical intimacy is welcomed in your marriage.

7. Keep the lines of communication open.

Grammy award-winning recording artist Michael W. Smith said it best in my book *All Pro Dad: Seven Essentials to Be a Hero to Your Kids*:

Communication has been the number one thing in our family. Just being able to communicate what you're feeling is so important. I think a lot of times families get in trouble when they stop communicating. Somebody gets his or her feelings hurt and then somebody gets defensive and then you just stop talking. You start doing that for long periods of time and the gap gets wider and it's just always harder to recover. It's always about communicating and keeping the lines of communication open with Deb and me in our marriage.

8. Play together.

Playing together creates oneness in marriage. Your play might include collecting things together. Maybe it's stamps, coins, or antiques. It could be you introducing her to fly fishing or her introducing you to gardening. Or find something that's new to both of you. In preparation for my father of the bride dance at my oldest daughter, Megan's, wedding, I had the joy of taking dance classes with her. It was so much fun that Susan and I are going to sign up to take classes together.

9. Speak kind words.

After many years of marriage, I noticed that I wasn't speaking kind words to my wife as much as I should. It's so easy to take the one we love for granted. So, I went back to the basics. When I wake up in the morning, I say, "Good morning, honey." When I arrive home, I ask, "How was your day?" When we go to bed, I pray with her and say "I love you" every single night.

10. Worship together.

I'm not just talking about singing, although that is important. Worship is about God being at the center of your life. Just as the earth revolves around the sun and keeps a constant orbit as a result of the gravitational pull of the sun, your life as a couple should constantly, day in and day out, revolve around God. As you attend church, pray, and grow in God together, you'll grow as one. I realize that opening your heart to God in front of your spouse might at first be a bit uncomfortable, but it's worth it. As you pray together, you'll get a front-row seat into one another's soul.

TAKING THE NEXT STEP

- Which one of these suggestions made you uncomfortable or maybe even cringe a little bit (or a lot)? Why do you think it caused a reaction?

  _____

  _____

- Do you feel that you have affair-proofed your marriage? After reading the above, are there any areas where you might be at risk?

  _____

  _____

- Think about it. What action can you take today to protect your marriage?

  _____

  _____

LIST 26

10 Questions to Ask Your Wife Every Year

We were on a trip with another family who were good friends. The other couple was so sweet to one another in both their affection and their words. We noticed that we really didn't interact in that way. We tended to be more direct with one another, and we wondered a little if there was something wrong with us. We wished we communicated a little more like them.

Soon thereafter, we were shocked when the wife filed for divorce. The husband said he was equally stunned. During the divorce proceedings the judge asked her the reason for her decision. She attempted to justify her actions by saying, "I'm just not happy." While they were sweet and affectionate with one another in public, they clearly weren't talking in private. Somewhere the pursuit of continually getting to know one another had stopped. They became disconnected.

You'll remember from List 20 that one of the most common mistakes men make in marriage is not knowing their wives. Good conversations lead to connection and intimacy. The best way to facilitate a good conversation is to ask great questions. Whether you feel like you know your wife well or not, the questions below will be helpful. The man who becomes an expert in the art of asking questions is the man who will win his wife's heart. Ask your wife these ten questions every year (or more often, if you'd like).

1. What are you enjoying most about our relationship right now?

Talking about what is going right will create optimism and renew energy. Tell her what you enjoy most about her.

2. What has been your biggest surprise in the last year?

This is a great way to gain insight into her expectations and the things she considers most important.

3. Where would you like our relationship to be this time next year?

It doesn't matter where you are, there's always room to be better. She might say, "I'd like to see more spontaneous affection." Or, "I want us to be moving forward together in our faith." She could say, "I want our relationship to involve more fun!"

4. How are you feeling about life in general?

Never assume you know how she is feeling. She may look okay on the surface, but be overwhelmed underneath. Don't just listen to what she says, but be sure to read between the lines as well.

5. What are your dreams for our future?

If you want to know what gets her up in the morning and what gives her hope, it's going to be this one. Find out her highest hopes for your future together. Give her the time to paint the picture for you.

6. If you could go anywhere, where would you go?

Let her imagination fantasize her ideal vacation. Get excited and dream with her. Maybe someday you can surprise her and make it a reality.

7. How do you think we're doing financially?

This needs to be an ongoing conversation. Just like a board of directors of a business meets at least annually to evaluate the finances and plan for the coming year, a husband and wife should do the same.

8. What do you want to do this year to improve our health?

Being in shape gives you more energy in everyday life. Encourage one another to exercise. It is a great activity to do together.

9. What is one thing you would change about how our family relates to one another?

This is one to brainstorm together. Set a vision of what a healthy family looks like, then model it. A few examples could be less TV, more constructive communication with less yelling, getting time away together, or eating dinner together more.

10. What is one thing I give my time to that you think would be better spent somewhere else?

You need to know where she wants your time. This will give her an open door to ask for it. It's an opportunity to see what she thinks is important.

TAKING THE NEXT STEP

- Think back to before you were married, when you and your wife were dating. Do you remember a conversation that could have lasted all night? What made it that way? Why were you so fascinated?

  _____

  _____

- What can you do to spark that interest again? Which one of these questions would be a great place to start today?

  _____

  _____

LIST 27

8 Secrets of Conflict Resolution

In the decades that followed World War II, serious tension existed between the United States and the Soviet Union. This was known as the Cold War. On Saturday, October 27, 1962, those tensions reached the brink of nuclear war. The Cuban Missile Crisis was in its terrorizing fourteenth day. Communication between President John F. Kennedy and Premier Nikita Khrushchev had been reduced to a naval game of cat and mouse.

On this particular day, the U.S. Navy repeatedly attempted to surface a Soviet submarine with depth charges. They were unaware that the sub was armed with nuclear warheads. The captain of the Soviet sub, furious and unable to communicate with Moscow, ordered the nuclear torpedoes battle ready. Fortunately, he was calmed down by his second captain, and a catastrophe was avoided. After realizing that quick and direct communication between the heads of state could have resolved the conflict before it escalated, they established a hotline for future situations.

Conflict with your wife can quickly escalate into a cold war. Poor communication, wrong assumptions, and handling disagreements immaturely can lead to eroded trust and disconnection. But when handled maturely conflict can be a healthy part of marriage. It's important to make sure that the hotline is always open. In his book *Learning to Live with the Love of Your Life... and Loving It!* Dr. Neil Clark Warren provides eight secrets to working through conflict with your wife.

1. "Recognize marriage as a 'we' business."

Dr. Warren says, "Any couple who gains a 'we' perspective eventually experiences great success in marriage." Shift the focus of your marriage to a "we" mentality, especially in conflict.

2. "Process the data as quickly as possible."

Deal with conflict by getting problems out in the open and addressing them head-on. Don't let issues fester below the surface.

3. "Stick to the subject."

If you are in the middle of an argument with your wife, stay focused on resolving that current conflict. Don't throw old fights or problems into the discussion.

4. "Don't intimidate."

Some people become more concerned with winning a fight than working through the conflict. They may become mean, intimidating, or threatening in order to stay in the fight. In Dr. Warren's words, "Intimidation may result in victory for an individual, but I've never seen it produce victory for the marriage."

5. "No name-calling."

Establish a rule with your wife that there will be no name-calling during a fight. Name-calling will only lead to more hurt and emotional distance between the two of you.

6. "Turn up your listening sensitivity."

While it may be hard to actively listen to your wife when your emotions are running high from an argument, you must take the time to try and see her point of view. This is key to the road to resolution. When your wife feels listened to, she will be more willing to listen to what you have to say as well.

7. "Practice give and take."

"What we must understand is that marriage is a partnership and therefore requires both give and take to be successful," says Dr. Warren. Be willing to compromise on certain issues that are more important to your wife. Choose your battles wisely.

8. "Celebrate every victory."

Recognize the victories when you and your wife successfully work through a conflict together. Focus on the progress you have made as a couple and the new strengths that you have together as a result.

TAKING THE NEXT STEP

- In which of the following four ways do you and your wife approach conflict? Why?

You   *Wife*

_____   _____ Passive—Avoid, avoid, avoid

_____   _____ Aggressive—Attack, control, and provoke

_____   _____ Passive-Aggressive—Surface agreement, secret undermining

_____   _____ Assertive—Honest, direct, clear

- From the above eight suggestions, what could you do to help make resolving conflict between you and your wife healthier and more productive?

_____

_____

- Ask your wife: What is one thing I do when we are having conflict that you would like me to change?

_____

_____

LIST 28

5 Kinds of Compliments to Give Your Wife

Mark Twain once said, "I can live for two months on a good compliment." I think that's universal. Everyone appreciates a good compliment.

That's *especially* true in marriage. A sincere, timely compliment can be a powerful difference maker for days. Likewise, when you criticize your wife, its effects can be felt for days and even weeks or months.

Increase and improve your compliments to your wife using these five types.

1. Relationship Skills: Compliment how she treats you and others.

This type of compliment starts with observing your wife. Note when she shows uncommon kindness, generosity, courtesy, or patience with you or anyone. Say something like "I really admire how kind you were to people in that crazy crowded store." Or, "You are really good at making me feel supported."

2. Parenting Skills: Compliment the way she handles your kids.

Your wife is more aware of her parenting mistakes than her parenting strengths. You can help her see what a positive difference she makes in your kids' lives. One time I sent Susan a quick text about how she was helping our daughters: "Susan, I just heard you talking with Megan and Emily, and you really coached them well on that issue. Great job!"

3. Get 'er Done Skills: Compliment her ability at a task.

It's important to let your wife know that you admire her abilities, but don't just compliment an extraordinary skill. Let her know you appreciate all the things she does by saying something like, "Thanks for cleaning the kitchen...I was tired and I really appreciated you doing that."

4. Challenges: Compliment her handling of a difficult situation.

If you see your wife navigate a hard situation well, let her know that you noticed. Tell her that you see how she helps your marriage and family. Perhaps say, "I know the last few days were unexpectedly difficult, but we couldn't have made it through without your steady hand. Thanks for keeping us calm."

5. Appearance or Style: Compliment the impression she makes on you.

If it's been a long time since you've complimented your wife, unprompted, about her appearance, do it this week. To be most effective, compliment how your wife improves what she wears, not vice versa. I sometimes say to my wife, "Susan, you make that dress look really good!"

TAKING THE NEXT STEP

- Write down three things about your wife you could compliment and then share those with her. Note her reaction and observe what types of compliments she enjoys most.

  _____

  _____

- Compliment Counter: How many compliments will you give your wife each day this week? Keep track below.

	Sunday	Monday	Tuesday	Wednesday	Thursday	Friday	Saturday
Compliment Count							

LIST 29

5 Ways Women Want Men to Take Initiative

A friend of ours has a wife who loves backpacking and camping. She was a former trail guide in Colorado. My friend, on the other hand, is the opposite of his wife. He likes to be in controlled environments. While they were still dating, they took a group of teenagers on a weeklong hiking and camping trip. Since our friend had little expertise, he assumed his wife, the expert, had everything covered, so he passively followed. He never offered to help, and to make matters worse, there were times when he had a less than positive attitude.

When the trip came to an end she was so upset that she literally did not talk to him for the entire four-hour flight home. His occasional bad attitude was reason enough, but what upset her so much was that he took no initiative to help lead. She felt completely alone, carrying the weight of the group by herself. Meanwhile, at the time, he thought everything was fine.

We have noticed that many people have relational difficulties due to a lack of initiative or perceived lack of initiative. When we sit passively rather than taking the lead or coming alongside our wives, everyone ends up frustrated.

Here are five common areas where women are looking for men to take initiative.

1. Vision and direction.

Women want men to set a standard and direction for the family. They desire us to point our families to a higher moral character. This is not to say they want things dictated to them. They are as much a part of determining the values of the family as us. However, they want us to carry the weight by living it out consistently, communicating it effectively, and reinforcing it.

2. Engagement.

Women want men that have eyes and ears for their family. They want full engagement and focus in conversation with both them and the kids. It's easy after a long day to want to check out. Remember that your family deserves, at the very least, as much attentive interest as you show at work. When you enter the front door, your spouse wants you to zero in on the family.

3. Planning.

Our wives want us to take initiative in planning things like vacations, date nights, family outings, and meals. We discussed this in List 20, "5 Common Mistakes Men Make in Marriage," with regard to thinking about our wives' needs. It makes them feel cared for when we think things through with them and help them plan. They feel even more cared for when we bring it up before they do. When we leave them alone to plan, they feel alone. That's the last thing we should want.

4. Home improvement.

We haven't met a woman yet who doesn't want a beautiful home. Right or wrong, in some ways, it is a representation of them. They want us to notice the small details they add to make the home look better and appreciate it. Carrying our share of responsibility for household cleaning is a way to take weight off their shoulders. However, probably the thing they want most from us is to dream with them about the ideal home. It's not really about size and wealth as much as it is creating a life together.

5. Finances.

Women want a sense of security. It's not about having a large salary but an understanding and clear picture of the financial details. Security comes by our driving the financial conversation, setting goals, and accountability. This doesn't mean dictating to them like a subordinate, but initiating the discussion about fiscal health. Then it involves strategizing with them on how to reach your agreed upon financial goals.

TAKING THE NEXT STEP

- Rate your initiative in these five areas. (Circle a number.)

1. **Vision and Direction**
   Weak   1   2   3   4   5   Strong

2. **Engagement**
   Weak   1   2   3   4   5   Strong

3. **Planning**
   Weak   1   2   3   4   5   Strong

4. **Home Improvement**
   Weak   1   2   3   4   5   Strong

5. **Finances**
   Weak   1   2   3   4   5   Strong

- Ask your wife which area she thinks is your strongest and which needs improvement. Make a note of her responses.

  _____

  _____

- What is one area that you will focus on improving in the next month?

  _____

  _____

LIST 30

3 Truths About You

Marriage is a humbling road that requires courage and steadfast, persistent love. It calls for forgiveness, grace, vulnerability, a denial of self, and commitment for life. What a former president of the United States, Teddy Roosevelt, said applies to a husband in marriage:

> It is not the critic who counts; not the man who points out how the strong man stumbles, or where the doer of deeds could have done them better. The credit belongs to the man who is actually in the arena, whose face is marred by dust and sweat and blood; who strives valiantly; who errs, who comes short again and again, because there is no effort without error and shortcoming; but who does actually strive to do the deeds;

who knows great enthusiasms, the great devotions; who spends himself in a worthy cause; who at the best knows in the end the triumph of high achievement, and who at the worst, if he fails, at least fails while daring greatly, so that his place shall never be with those cold and timid souls who neither know victory nor defeat.

As you *dare greatly* in the *great devotion* of loving your wife well, it is important to remember a couple of important truths about yourself. Remember these particularly when you are feeling down, isolated, or hopeless.

1. You are valuable for who you are, not for what you do.

You were created exclusively by God and for God. And because of that, you are immeasurably valuable. There were no flaws in your design and no errors in your construction. You are handmade, custom designed, and fully loaded by God.

2. You have gifts—embrace them.

Every person has gifts or strengths. If you don't know yours, we'd encourage you to ask five family members and friends this question, "In one or two words, what do you think is my single greatest strength?" They'll all probably give you similar answers. Those answers identifying your area of giftedness will help you understand the truth that you have a lot to offer your family and the world.

3. You weren't meant to do this alone.

If you're constantly putting on a front that you have it all together, other people will start to believe that you really do have it all together. So, we challenge you to be honest with trusted friends and family. Share your struggles with them and let them help carry your burdens and encourage you. Because the truth is: you were *never* meant to do this alone.

Now continue *in the arena, strive valiantly*, and never stop pursuing the *worthy cause* of loving your wife well. You are one with her. Give her 100 percent. Resist temptation. Pursue holiness. Love her for better or worse, for life.

TAKING THE NEXT STEP

- What good gifts do you bring into your marriage? How does your wife benefit from them? Ask your wife what she thinks your gifts are.

  _____

  _____

- What gifts does your wife bring to the marriage? How do your differing gifts complement each other?

  _____

  _____

CONCLUSION:
SURGING FORWARD

Congratulations on completing the thirty lists! What you have just accomplished took a great amount of courage and commitment. At the beginning of the book, I told you about my own transformation and how I am a different husband today from when I first started. I mentioned that every day I try to take another step toward having a better marriage. There have been days where I have made huge gains. There have also been discouraging days where I have felt like I gained only a yard or perhaps even stepped backward. Remember, though, that God has called us to love our wives well, no matter what their response. Never stop that pursuit. It may take consistency over time before you see results. It's like something Dale Carnegie said: *Most of the important things in the world have been accomplished by people who have kept on trying when there seemed to be no hope at all.*

So the question is, how did you do? Did you move the ball down the field? We want to encourage you that even if you moved the ball only a little bit forward, that is something to feel good about. It means that you have improved as a husband. It means that your wife is being more loved today than she was yesterday. We would recommend repeating the process of reading these lists to love by and adding new things to improve upon. We think you'll find yourself gaining momentum as you consistently love your wife well. Now continue forward and build on the work you have started. Taking small steps today will mean getting closer to the marriage you want tomorrow.

ACKNOWLEDGMENTS

The truths in this book are not our own. So we must tell you that the Author of these truths, and all truth, is God Himself. He is truth. And He is worthy of our standing ovation, moment by moment, day by day.

Through our married life, many, many people have spoken into our lives. And while they may not have penned any of the words in this book, we consider them to be co-authors with us. Our children, now all in their twenties, have had a front-row seat in our marriage. Knowing that Megan, Emily, Hannah, Mark Jr., and Grant were always watching inspired us to work really hard in our relationship. And we salute Army Captain Hampton Tignor, who recently married our Megan and now serves our country as a judge advocate general (JAG). You are an inspiration to us. We are also very grateful to our parents for teaching us the importance of family.

We applaud the talented BJ Foster. With great flexibility and ability, BJ spent many hours working with us brainstorming, organizing, and editing the content in this book. And to our team at Family First, we say a big "thank you!" We are honored to stand with you as we strive to be a voice of truth for families.

Once again, we put our hands together for our faithful literary agent, DJ Snell. His gracious style and encouragement have been embraced by us through the process of producing this work.

Our editors Joey Paul and Becky Hughes, Patsy Jones and Andrea Glickson in marketing, art director Jody Waldrup, and editorial/production manager Bob Castillo, we shine the spotlight on you and the FaithWords team for your service to us and to all the married couples who, through this book, will be inspired to love one another well.

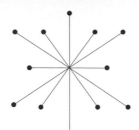

STAY
CONNECTED
Continue the journey to loving well.

CONNECT
with Susan

🌐 BLOG: www.susan.me

f facebook.com/susanmerrill

🐦 twitter.com/susan_merrill

📷 instagram.com/susanmerrill

📌 pinterest.com/susan_merrill

READ
Susan's book

📖 *The Passionate Mom—Dare to Parent in Today's World*

CONNECT
with Mark

🌐 BLOG: www.markmerrill.com

f facebook.com/markmerrill

🐦 twitter.com/markmerrill

📷 instagram.com/markmerrill

READ
Mark's book

📖 *All Pro Dad—Seven Essentials to Be a Hero to Your Kids*

LISTEN

 The Family First Podcast with Mark & Susan Merrill (iTunes)

WATCH

 Mark and Susan Merrill (YouTube)

EXPLORE
our programs

 **Family First** |

Mark and Susan are the founders of Family First, a national non-profit organization. The mission of Family First is to provide parenting, marriage and relational truth that helps people love their family well and gives them greater hope for the future. We do this through the following programs.

 All Pro Dad is a program to help dads love and lead their families well. We provide practical resources to dads through events in NFL stadiums, dads and kids breakfast programs, and online at allprodad.com.

 iMOM is a program to help moms love and nurture their families well. Being a mom is hard! We inspire and encourage moms to be the best they can be by providing resources that help online at imom.com.

 The Family Minute with Mark Merrill is a daily radio feature that offers advice on marriage, parenting and family relationships. The Family Minute is heard on over 350 radio stations in 46 states and globally on American Forces Network.
